# • MODERN PALMISTRY •

# • MODERN PALMISTRY •

*A unique guide to hand analysis*

## SASHA FENTON
## &
## MALCOLM WRIGHT

Sterling Publishing Co., Inc.
New York
A Sterling/Zambezi Book

Library of Congress Cataloging-in-Publication Data Available

10 9 8 7 6 5 4 3 2 1

Published in 2003 by Sterling Publishing Co., Inc.
387 Park Avenue South, New York NY 10016
© 2003 by Sasha Fenton and Malcolm Wright
Distributed in Canada by Sterling Publishing
$^{c}$/o Canadian Manda Group, One Atlantic Avenue
Toronto, Ontario, Canada M6K 3E7
Distributed in Australia by Capricorn Link (Australia) Pty. Ltd.
P.O. Box 704, Windsor, NSW 2756 Australia

Sterling ISBN 1-4027-0482-8

# Contents

# Disclaimer

This book will be on sale in many countries around the world, and sadly, it is a fact of life nowadays that there are a few people around who try to get rich by harassing others where one law or another leaves a loophole, so there is a parallel need to avoid such problems. The alternative would be never to write non-fiction books at all!

This book is designed to provide information in regard to the subject matter covered. It is sold with the understanding that the publisher and the author are not engaged in rendering legal, accounting, advisory or any other professional services in this book, and cannot be held responsible for the outcome if any of the contents are used for any purpose whatsoever. If expert assistance is required in connection with any subject matter covered within this book, the services of a competent professional should be sought.

It is not the purpose of this book to reprint all the information that is otherwise available to the author and/or publisher, but to complement, amplify and supplement other texts. You are urged to read all the available material, learn as much as possible about the subject matter and to tailor the information to your individual needs.

Palmistry is not a get-rich-quick scheme. Anyone who decides to make a career out of the application of any divinatory systems must expect to invest a lot of time, effort and resources. Also, the spiritual aspect of such work ensures that it should never be seen solely in terms of moneymaking.

Every effort has been made to make this book as complete and accurate as possible within the limitations of size and content. However, there may be mistakes, both typographical and in content. Therefore, this text should be used only as a general guide and not as an ultimate source of data on the subject matter concerned. Furthermore, only information known to the author and/or publisher up to the printing date is included.

The purpose of this book is to educate and entertain. The author and/or publisher shall have neither liability nor responsibility to any person or entity with respect to any loss or damage caused, or alleged to be caused, directly or indirectly by the information contained in this book.

If you do not wish to be bound by the above, you may return this book to the publisher for a full refund.

## Dedication

For our families

# INTRODUCTION

We have written this book for those who are interested in hand reading and want a more up-to-date approach to the subject. The ideas
presented here have come directly from our own experience of
working with hands. We have attempted to explain how character
and personality can be read and how this information can be con-
structively used by the reader to understand his own nature and to
help others to get to grips with theirs in order to get more out of life.
Incidentally, we have decided for the sake of convenience to use the
masculine terms of "he" and "him" throughout this book.

## History of Hand Analysis

Hand analysis, more commonly known as palmistry, goes back to the
dawn of time, and it is truly amazing that so many hand readers from
different cultures and different centuries actually agree on so many
aspects of hand analysis. One of those who gave birth to modern methods was Casimir Stanislas d'Arpentigny who classified hand shapes into
the now famous types of spatulate, square, elementary, conic, psychic,
philosophic and mixed. The French nobleman Adrien Adolphe
Desbarrolles had a mystical view of hand reading that he wrapped up
with other occult ideas. He gave daily consultations in his apartment in
the strangely named Rue d'Enfer (Road of Hell). He also studied
graphology and phrenology and was deeply convinced that the Kabbala
was the center of all wisdom and guidance for the soul, mind and body.

Another famous name in palmistry was Count Louis Hamon (1866
–1936), better known as Cheiro, who studied hand analysis for over forty
years, along with other occult research work, such as numerology and
astrology. He taught and lectured, traveling widely in Europe and
America, amazing the VIPs of his day with the accuracy of his readings.

## Clairvoyance

Hand analysis is a science and does not need to rely on intuition.
People who read hands will find themselves developing intuitively as

well as developing knowledge of psychology and human behavior. The actual act of hand reading means that one sits with the client in a quiet room building up a relaxed and trusting atmosphere. This will open the door to clairvoyant faculties in much the same way as meditation and yoga can do. It is not possible to work as a professional hand reader without learning to understand people—so in time, even the most "scientific" hand reader learns to use that inexplicable intuitive nudge that comes while working on a hand.

## Interpretation

Hands vary much more than one imagines and there must be some leeway for interpretation. Skilled hand analysts do use varying interpretations, in the same way that astrologers vary in their opinions. In some cases we ourselves have different ways of interpreting the same lines or different ways of coming to the same conclusion, and where that occurs, we give both our opinions.

Some lines give information on more than one aspect of one's life, in the same way that a sign of the Zodiac can encompass a wide variety of ideas within itself. These lines will have to be read carefully with due attention being paid to other parts of the hand. Wherever we have to deal with this kind of problem we will give a detailed cross reference—we will not just say vaguely "other areas of the hand will have to be looked at."

Beginners and advanced hand readers alike will find something to interest them in our book because the information within it ranges from the basics to the most advanced techniques. We have not tried to turn traditional palmistry on its head, indeed we have followed the traditional ideas where we have found them to work well and if any of our opinions differ from the usual ones, it is because our conclusions have grown out of our personal research. Where methods are so recent that they have not had time to be conclusively researched, we are throwing these over to you to test against your own clients. We make a point of explaining our reasoning so that the reader can see the logic behind the new theories. We hope that our departures from the traditional and "official" line will bring many hours of happy argument and research to the world of hand analysis.

# Illustrations

Up to now many hand-reading books have been spoiled by the fact that they have either been illustrated by artists who are not hand readers or hand readers who cannot draw, but in this book we are lucky to be able to draw upon Malcolm's background and knowledge. Thankfully, he not only has many years of hand-reading experience behind him but also a long career as a technical illustrator. In addition to being an illustrator, he is also a creative artist who has successfully sold his own paintings.

Each illustration has been carefully prepared to give a clear and accurate picture, often backed up by hand prints, in order to show precisely what we have described in the text. All the diagrams are drawn as if looking at the right hand print of a right-handed person. The inked prints are all right handed unless otherwise stated.

We hope that you will give yourself time to absorb the ideas and gradually work your way through the case histories. This book should give you a thorough grounding in the art of hand analysis.

# How to Take Prints

## Equipment
- Water-based printing ink, available from art shops.
- Rubber roller, also from an art shop.
- Ceramic tile or a dinner plate that you no longer use.
- Paper kitchen towel.
- Plain white paper—office photocopy paper is ideal.
- An old rolling pin.

## Method
Squeeze a little of the ink onto the tile and then roll it onto the roller. Lightly roll off any excess onto the kitchen towel. Gently roll the ink onto the hand, being careful not to press it deeply into the lines on the hand. Place the hand on the paper and press gently so that all of the hand is in contact with the paper. If the hand is very hollow in the middle, then place the paper on the rolling pin and roll the hand over it. This will distort the appearance of the fingers, therefore it would be a good idea to do one set of prints with the roller and one without, thereby getting the whole of the palm on paper and also having a separate set of prints with the fingers correctly shown. Alternatively, experiment with hard and soft surfaces placed under the paper.

# CHAPTER ONE

# BASIC INFORMATION

## Size of Hands

The hands should be in proportion to the size of the body. If they are exceptionally large, the subject may be very slow and cautious, and if very small, either very fast-moving and excitable or totally idle. Either way there will be an imbalance in the personality and probably an unhappy nature.

## Hand Shapes

These give an "at a glance" clue to character. One should let common sense be one's guide, after all a large square, heavily callused hand is hardly likely to belong to an accountant.

## The Mounts (Fig. 1.1)

This is the basic "map" of the palm. The areas that are known as mounts each have their own character. This gives a brief introduction to the mounts.

### Jupiter

Ambition, application of will power, dignity, financial drives, religious and philosophic outlook.

### Saturn

Practicalities, work, materialism, responsibility, search for truth, science.

### Apollo

Home, relationships, hobbies, arts and crafts, and self-expression.

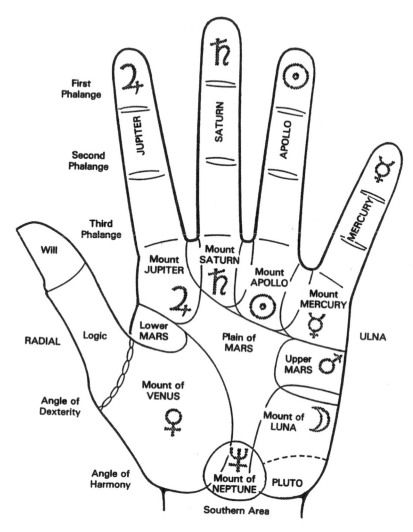

Figure 1.1   The Mounts

## Mercury
Communications, business, health, relationships, family, interests, diplomacy, honesty.

## Lower Mars
Military matters, courage, resistance.

## Upper Mars
Courage, temper, resilience, persistence, restlessness, drive.

## Venus
Home, family, love, music, art, possessions, values, sensuality, stamina.

## Neptune
Link between conscious and unconscious, health, intuition.

## Luna
Travel, imagination, intuition, outdoor hobbies, freedom.
Each finger draws energy from its adjacent mount.

# Major Lines (Fig. 1.2)

## Life line
The way one lives, health, drive, location of home, travel, efforts and failures.

## Head line
The mind, mental and physical health, career, and education.

## Heart line
Health, feelings, sexuality, and outlook on relationships.

## Fate line
Work, earned money, partnerships, successes and failures.

## Apollo line
Home, family, hobbies, interests, arts, and relationships.

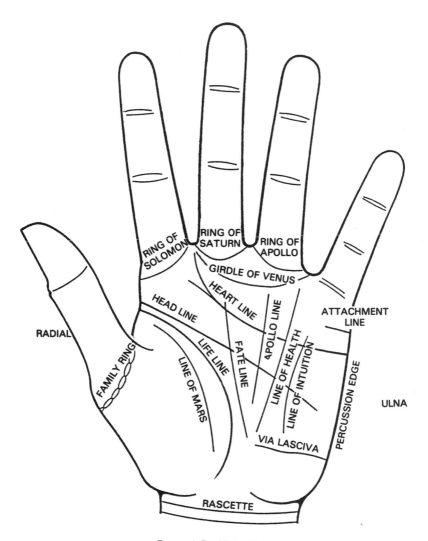

Figure 1.2   Major Lines

## Minor Lines

There are too many to go into detail in this section. Most people will have a few minor lines but probably not all of them. Lines that are frequently found are the attachment/relationship lines, child lines and travel lines.

## Marks

Crosses, grilles etc. The old-time palmists seem to have put a great deal of stock by these marks, but we do not think that most of them are terribly important; however they do appear when something is on the subject's mind and some can be a valuable guide. Especially interesting ones are squares of restriction/protection and crosses of irritation. Other marks are actual patterns that lie under the skin, such as finger prints. These do not change much in adulthood, and they give information on personality and particular talents.

## Hard/Soft Hands

Firmness in hands indicates good health and a resourceful, self-reliant, tough personality, someone who is hard on himself and on others. Soft hands belong to gentler people who need to lean on others. Illness will make the hands soft, as will old age, pregnancy and vegetarianism. Hands that feel like a wet sponge trapped in a plastic bag show that something is very wrong.

## Color

Pale hands indicate a limp and unenthusiastic personality whereas very red hands are traditionally supposed to mean bad temper. However, color is mainly to do with health. Pale hands could indicate anemia, yellow ones jaundice, gray/blue ones heart trouble, red patches on Luna overactive thyroid or high blood-pressure, blue/white poor circulation. (See more about this in the chapter on health.)

## Flexibility

Flexible hands are found on people who become bored easily. They need to have a stimulating job where they are offered a variety of problems and challenges plus plenty of sporting or social life. These people need to feel fairly free but are *not* necessarily particularly adaptable. The person whose fingers offer absolutely no resistance may be too dependent on the goodwill of others.

Inflexible hands show people who want a steady job and a quiet routine at home. They do not seek popularity and may be too

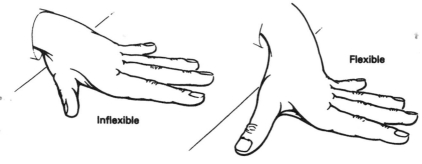

Figure 1.3    Flexible Hands

unbending toward others. They cannot cope too well with unexpected events; they prefer to know where they are from one day to the next.

## The Dominant Hand

*Length of days is in her right hand; and in her left hand riches and honor*
Proverbs 3.16.

The gypsies in Spain charge a fee to read one hand and double the amount to read both but a reading with only one hand is a complete waste of time. The length of days and the events that take place are marked on the right hand. The inner desires and the potential for gaining riches and honor are marked on the left. One must establish which is the dominant, or major, hand. Normally it is the one used to write with. In the case of a left-handed person, both hands must be studied. Take note of any differences in the hands concerning events in the past, and then give the interpretation of these events to the subject. The feedback from this gives a clue to the dominant hand. Sometimes more fine "worry" lines can be seen on the minor hand than on the dominant one. Even armed with this information, it would be best to proceed with caution.

The dominant hand is reality. It is what we make of our lives plus our conscious self, the side we show to the outside world. It is also our achievements, the way we plan our lives, our changing views of relationships, work and money. It is the down-to-earth side of life. The major lines of Life, Head and Heart on the dominant hand also represent the physical organs of the body.

## The Minor Hand

This hand represents our inner, unconscious self. This is the side that we hide from others. It could be called the "I wish" hand because it represents our inner aspirations the way we would like life to be rather than the reality we have to live with.

The lines of Life, Head and Heart on the minor hand represent the nervous, emotional and sexual energies of the body. This is where the build-up of nervous energies will appear before they arrive in the form of an impending physical illness on the dominant hand (see Chapter 12).

## Marked Differences Between Left and Right Hands

Marked differences between the hands can lead to mental, physical or sexual difficulties. For instance, if the radial end of the heart line peters out on the mount of Jupiter on one hand and between Saturn and Jupiter on the other, this person will always question love. He or she will have difficulties in understanding himself physically and psychologically. A rigid Saturn finger on the dominant hand and a flexible Saturn finger on the minor hand would imply a wish to be seen doing the right thing, and an inner desire to throw caution to the winds.

Differences in the formation of the head line between the two hands lead to a peculiar form of psychosis or split personality. In some cases the subject has trained himself to behave in a manner which is acceptable to his family or co-workers while he is inwardly longing to act differently.

## Size Differences

In many cases one hand (usually the dominant one) is larger than the other is. This shows growth of confidence and capability due to coping with life. If the dominant hand is obviously squarer, it shows an increase in practicality during the subject's life.

There are cases where the lines on the minor hand show past experiences that appear to have been traumatic, but despite the apparent scale of these events, the lines do not seem to appear on the dominant hand. When these lines are pointed out to the subject and the possible course of past events is discussed, he usually confirms that he went through a bad patch in the past, but he has put it behind him now and cannot really recall the pain of it any more. This is quite normal, as the memory *must* become insensitive to painful past events for the sake of mental health. We may learn from the past, but cannot go through life with the pain undiminished—and the hands show this.

## Full Hands (Fig. 1.4)

Full hands have a cobweb of fine lines; they belong to people who are highly strung and liable to become upset and over-emotional at

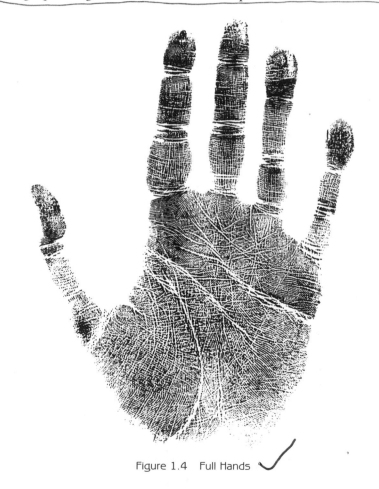

Figure 1.4   Full Hands

the drop of a hat. Tense and anxious, people with this type of personality live on their nerves, constantly expecting things to go wrong. Their imagination is so highly developed that they see problems where none exist and try to cross bridges before coming to them. Their nervous and emotional energies are near the surface, and they learn about life the hard way. They may distrust those who are around them and blame them for their own weakness.

These hands inflict a degree of sensitivity, which makes life an uncomfortable experience. The positive side is creative or artistic talent. If there is also a long head line the subject will be sympathetic and very caring toward others. Unless there is a strong Apollo line, this person will lack the courage, confidence, tenacity and luck required to carry out his schemes.

The biggest problem is unnecessary worry. The subject is suspended in a form of mental paralysis between desires and fears, so the energies become dissipated and arrive in force as fine worry lines on the hand. These people require a creative outlet in order to avoid becoming frustrated. Routine jobs bore them; they must have variety if they are not to become restless. They hate to be confined but may also be afraid of large spaces and crowds of people. These are difficult hands.

## Patchy Hands

If only the mount of Luna is covered in lines, the subject will be nervous of travelling and will only feel comfortable when close to home, where he can keep an eye on his property and family. This type of marking is found on hands that have a characteristic inward dent on the percussion side at the base of the mount of Luna. If the area around the heart line, especially under the area of Saturn, is covered in fine lines, the subject is not at ease in his personal and romantic relationships. If lines extend out onto the palm from inside Venus, there is family aggravation of one kind or another. This may take the form of practical problems or it may indicate an overly critical attitude by a parent or spouse.

## Health and the Full Hand

Full hands belong to nervous people who can literally make themselves ill with tension and anxiety. They may suffer from migraines, insomnia or 101 other ailments. However, when the chips are down, these people can sometimes cope better than their calmer "empty-handed" friends can.

The empty hand has few lines on the palm surface, just the four major lines and one or two others. Some of these people are relatively calm and can cope with most things. They do not worry about other people's opinion of them; they are self-confident, practical and even-tempered. Thinking is logical if rather slow, unimaginative unless there is a long sloping head line, and the reasoning powers are good because they are unclouded by emotion. They could be critical toward others. If these people have short fingers they would

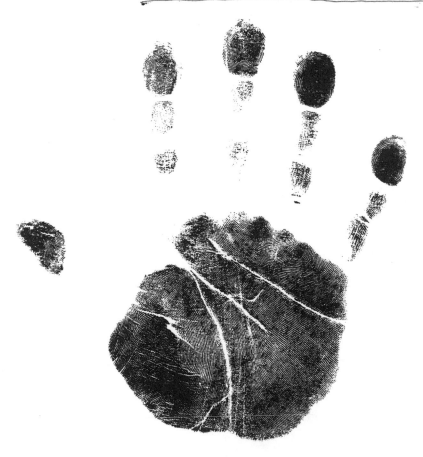

Figure 1.5   Empty Hands

relegate sex to a rather boring weekly routine; romance would not mean much to them. If in addition the head line were straight and fairly short, then the subject would see things in shades of black and white, missing all the subtleties of life.

## Health and the Empty Hand (Fig. 1.5)

One would think that someone with an empty hand would be cool, calm and collected, but this is not so, because a person who finds life especially difficult can have an empty hand. There is no outlet in emotional or neurotic behavior, so these subjects can go down with a terrible bang under severe stress. They may take to drugs or drink, smoke and eat too much or they may just become ill.

# CHAPTER TWO

# THE HAND

## Hand Shapes

Most people become defeated by some of the old hand-shape termi-
nology. Who can sort out a philosophic hand from a psychic with the
aid of the average palmistry book? Here we have given some descriptions that should match up to reality.

## Square Hands (Fig. 2.1)

These hands are of equal width
at both the base and the finger
ends. They belong to practical,
rational people who prefer to
live an ordinary life. These people like to finish what they start
and are not easily bored. We
cannot live without these types;
they do what is required and
they like routines and systems.
They usually have only the
major lines on the hand and
these will be clear cut and fairly
straight on a surface that is firm
and warm to the touch. There
are probably more men with
this type of hand than women,
but in either sex they are sensible, fairly resourceful and
financially sound, good business people and good family
folk.

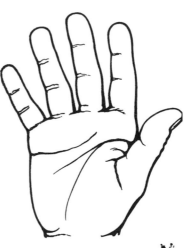

Figure 2.1   Square hand

## Short Wide (Elementary) Hands (Fig. 2.2)

These hands are short and rather squat with square finger ends and a short thumb. The lines are short and straight showing an inability to express feelings. Very elementary hands are found on mentally handicapped people, in which case they show an inability to live life to the fullest. When this is not the case, these people are just rather dense and pedestrian. The short-wide-handed person is best suited to a very basic practical job. He doesn't like change or new methods and ideas. There is a possibility of a somewhat violent temper as "elementary" people have difficulty in expressing themselves verbally.

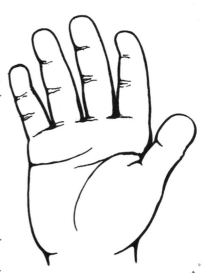

Figure 2.2 Elementary hand

## Rounded Elegant (Conic) Hands (Fig. 2.3)

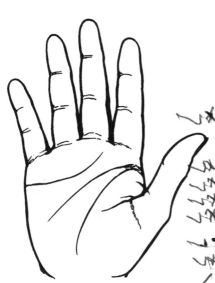

Figure 2.3 Conic hand

The shape is gently rounded and rather pleasant to look at. It indicates a fairly gentle, idealistic, sensitive nature with a strong creative streak. Although too energetic to be classed as dreamers, there is a dreamy, romantic side to these people. They need comfort, and even a measure of luxury, and they have a fairly optimistic outlook. The hand should be fairly firm and springy and the lines gently curving. There could be artistic leanings, and these subjects certainly enjoy the results of other people's artistic creations. Warm-hearted people

practical & creative outlets!
Cooking! crafts? singing; the arts! gardening;
The Hand   **17**

with a liking for peace and family
life, they are good at practical tasks
as long as they also have a creative
element in them. They are helpful,
preferring to follow than to lead,
quite resourceful, usually sensible
and humorous. On a bad day, they
can be irritable, unreasonable and
oversensitive. Their greatest need
is for good personal relationships.

## Small Soft Hands
## (Fig. 2.4)

These people obviously do not do
any kind of manual work. They try
as much as possible to lead an easy

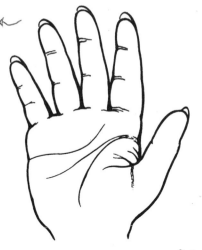

Figure 2.4   Small soft hand

life without having to expend too much physical effort. They can be
surprisingly canny in business, and it is amazing how frequently this
type of hand turns up on a person who has a wide-eyed look of total
innocence that hides a surprisingly active mind. They are takers
rather than givers. The lines are mainly fine but clearly etched, rather
straight and often made up from broken lines (especially the heart
line). At best these small soft hands may have
pointed fingers that indicate artistic appreciation and a love of beauty. If the hands are
tipped with fat little finger ends and shovel-
shaped nails that seem to lift up from the fingers, then beware; these people may look all
innocence but they can be *very* manipulative
indeed and extremely selfish.

## Claw-like Hands (Fig. 2.5)

Such hands may indicate a greedy grasping
nature, a person who can see *only* his own
needs and is not prepared to see any other
person's point of view. We have seen these
hands on clients who are waiting for their
partners to die so that they can have the ben-

Figure 2.5   Claw-like hand

efit of their goods or money without

the bother of having to care for them any longer. The lines may be weak and sloppy or quite strongly etched, but the mounts are rather flat (with the possible exception of Jupiter) and the whole hand is cramped in appearance with a large hollow in the middle. The nails are likely to be long and narrow, and if they also curve like claws, there is an extremely selfish, greedy or grasping personality. The skin surface often has a crumpled appearance and if the palmist gently makes a dent in the surface when the hand is relaxed, the dent will stay there until the hand is stretched and used once more! These people rarely go out to work, as they are not interested in either a career for themselves or, heaven forbid, helping others in any way. If they do have to work, they make life a misery for all their colleagues as they are only in it for what they can get and have no time for the social niceties.

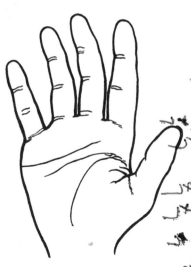

Figure 2.6   A-shaped hand

## A-Shaped (Spatulate) Hands (Fig. 2.6)

A-shaped hands are narrow at the base and wider at the finger ends. This is an independent energetic type who has an original way of looking at life. He needs a physical or sporting outlet, but most of all the A-shape type needs mental challenges and problems to get his or her teeth into. He could be a craftsman, inventor or even writer, but he enjoys going out into the open air, or out onto water from time to time. These subjects could be good around the farm, as they are unlikely to be scared of large animals.

## V-Shaped (Spatulate) Hands (Fig. 2.7)

This subject is also inventive but probably less of a craftsman. Either type of spatulate subject is highly ambitious. He may adopt an abrupt and hasty manner towards slower people who get in his way. There is a great need for physical activity, as this person finds it hard to sit

still and wants to make the most of every opportunity in life. These people enjoy a challenge and need an outlet in vigorous sports—this is the successful tennis or squash player. These highly strung, energetic types would make enthusiastic practical scientists, geographers or explorers.

## Knotty or Knobbly Hands (Philosophic) (Fig. 2.8)

These hands belong to intellectual types who live in the realm of ideas. They are pleasant, good company, interesting to talk with and also appreciate creativity. They enjoy the company of their family, but neither

Figure 2.7   V-shaped hand

sex is terribly practical around the home. They can be easily sidetracked by an interesting discussion, a good book or a fascinating word game with the children. Those readers who are interested in astrology might see these people as being Aquarian types. The lines on these hands are usually well formed, gently curving but not too deeply etched.

## Long Narrow Hands (Fig. 2.9)

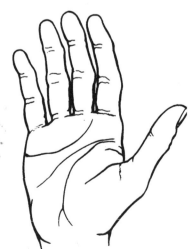

These people lack balance and common sense. They may be pretty sharp artistically but their rather inward-looking, self-centered nature makes it difficult for them to relate comfortably to others. They lack practicality and are probably better off working quietly at home. They find other people rather hard to cope with at times. They do not have much physical strength or stamina. The hands may have rather thin and reedy lines. If there is a network of very fine lines,

Figure 2.8   Knotty or knobbly hand

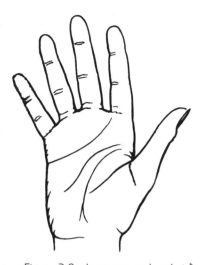

Figure 2.9   Long narrow hand

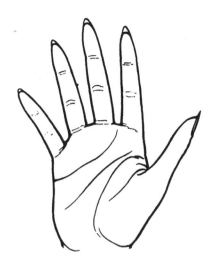

Figure 2.10   Long delicate hand

they will be oversensitive and nervy. They may think highly of themselves and put on airs and graces.

## Long Delicate Hands (Psychic) (Fig. 2.10)

These hands have slim tapering fingers, a straight thin thumb and smooth-looking fingers. These people are sensitive and imaginative, possibly artistic too. Their feelings are very near the surface—they can be easily hurt and can identify with other people's suffering. There is a tendency to over-dramatize themselves and play the martyr until something comes along to distract their attention. They fall deeply in love and may suffer from unrequited love, because they are shy about revealing their feelings. They may be embarrassed about sexual matters. They will suffer disappointments in life because their standards are unrealistically high.

## Monkey-Like Hands (Fig. 2.11)

Such hands have slim, grasping fingers. These people are talented, quick, clever and somewhat slippery and untrustworthy.

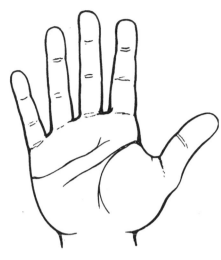

Figure 2.11   Monkey-like hand

## Short, Plump, Energetic Hands

There is a certain type of small hand that is sometimes rather "full" but not soft to the touch. These people are energetic and rather proud. They make good spouses but, possibly, rather impatient parents. The lines on these hands tend to curve and the rather full mounts show warmth of character, but the characteristically small A-shaped (spatulate) fingernails and rather bluey-mauve color point to a good deal of personal ambition.

## Square Slim Hands

These folk are practical, decisive, energetic, honest, straightforward and good natured. They do not like to let any one down. Living with this type means being prepared for an energetic relationship, sharing in his or her ideas and enthusiasms.

## Short Wide Hands

These people have fingers that taper towards the tips. The thumb may bend a long way back and curve outwards. Practical and realistic but with a really terrific sense of humor, this type will place a high value on humor in friends of either sex. They are creative, generous and helpful and also good with their hands. They are very sociable and put this to good use when trying to form relationships.

## A Large Thumb

A large thumb could be either straight or bent, giving the hand a lopsided look. Ambitious and competitive, these people tackle life energetically, whether it is work, hobbies or school exams. They are so single-minded that they usually get what they want.

## Mixed Hands

Some hands defy categorization, and will be a mixture of any of the types that we have already mentioned, or they may be in a class of their own. Basically, if the radial side is more developed, then the subject will be energetic in worldly matters, while if the ulna side is stronger, they are more home-loving and imaginative. A square palm with long fingers indicates a practical artist, illustrator, dressmaker, etc., while a long square palm with short conic fingers denotes an enthusiastic quick-thinking and quick-acting person, who despite appearanes has the application to finish what he starts and to make a good job of it.

## Radial/Ulna Sides of the Hand (Fig. 2.12)

The radial side is the thumb side and the ulna side is the edge or percussion side of the hand. Some palmists use the system shown in Fig. 2.12a, others prefer the system as per Fig. 2.12b.

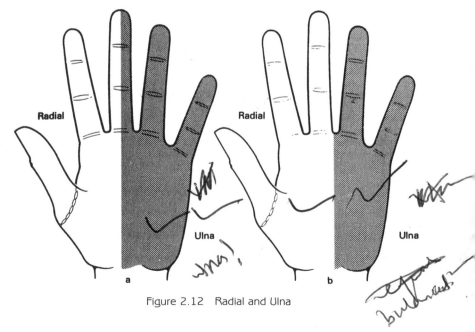

Figure 2.12    Radial and Ulna

## Radial (Fig. 2.12)

This is concerned with the outer personality. It could be termed masculine or active, and if well developed shows that the subject copes well with worldly affairs. A well-developed radial side would make for someone who is practical and businesslike, and who may be executive material. He is comfortable with any situation that requires assertion, confidence and a sense of personal authority. The subject will be sexually active, possibly rather demanding and will have a strong desire to live life to the fullest.

## Ulna (Fig. 2.12)

This is concerned with the inner personality: feminine, intuitive and receptive. If this side is well developed, the subject is highly imaginative and may use this imagination as part of his work or to enrich his life. This person will be sympathetic. He will be gentle, caring and pleasant, and he will get on well with children and animals, and have a love of art, music and all creative work.

## The Importance of Balance

In palmistry, everything depends on balance. Too much of one thing on a hand will cause that person to be overdeveloped in one area of life and lacking in some of the others. If a hand appears to be lopsided, then we suggest that you take a piece of paper and cover up half of the hand and see what you would have if the missing half looked the same as the half you can still see; then change halves. This can give an astonishing picture of two people in one.

If the radial side is heavier, the subject will be active, competitive, materialistic, and capable in worldly matters but could find difficulty in expressing or understanding feelings. Too much ulna is rare but when it does occur, it implies a personality that is awash with emotion and imagination, longing to be creative but lacking the drive to do so. Obviously the subject with a hand which is balanced and fairly even on both sides will not have either trait too strongly marked. If the hand is generally weak looking, then neither the assertive and capable nor the creative and sensitive side will be developed and a kind of peevish selfishness will take over. If the hand is generally strong and firm then the personality has a nice balance between action and reception, creativity and scientific ability, understanding and action.

## Mounts (Fig. 1.1)

Perhaps we should think of the mounts as the names of countries and seas that appear on a map. They may not have too much importance in themselves, but each one has its own character, and this must be borne in mind when looking at the lines that touch them and the marks which appear on them. They are *all* called mounts, even Neptune and Saturn that often look more like valleys. The mounts of Jupiter, Saturn, Apollo and Mercury are the energy reserves of the fingers.

## The Radial Mounts

### Jupiter

This represents the practical use of will power, ambition and pride. If well developed it confers executive ability, strong personal beliefs, even religious beliefs, plus the desire for and ability to use authority. If overdeveloped, the person is arrogant, over-ambitious, selfish, a bully or a bigot. If underdeveloped there is not much ambition or personal dignity plus a dislike of authority.

### Venus

This represents love, both the type of affection one has for family and friends and, to some extent, sexual love. If full and firm the subject will have plenty of energy and stamina and will live life to the full. He will enjoy music, dancing, beauty and the arts, a good meal and a night out. He will probably have a good sense of humor. A high Venus mount suggests a zest for life and a great deal of desire, but this desire can be for material goods or for an abstract idea rather than simply for sex.

If the mount is full but soft, this can indicate a person who is self-indulgent, lazy and greedy. A cramped small mount signifies a person who, apart from lacking in physical stamina, would be cold and over-concerned with the practicalities of life to the exclusion of enjoyment. This type could be selfish, unsympathetic, mean, unloving and in an odd way, domineering.

## Lower Mars

It might help the reader to think of lower Mars as being the attacking force, upper Mars being tenacity in defense. We sometimes see a really high lower Mars on military hands, also on those who have made a hobby out of scouting or some such paramilitary organization. If fairly large, the subject is assertive, capable, something of a go-getter. If almost missing, he would sit and whine rather than go out and do something to change his situation.

## The Balance Mounts

These are neither radial nor ulna; they hold the balance between the inner and outer sides of the personality.

## Saturn

This mount is concerned with practical ambitions, earned money, serious thought, scientific investigation, solitude, practical gains but emotional limitations. If large or obvious, there could be a gloomy, pessimistic, solitary attitude to life, and the subject would be cautious or easily depressed.

## Neptune

This is the bridge between Venus and Luna—or, in other terms, the conscious and the unconscious drives. If the mount is equal in height with Venus and Luna, the subject is sympathetic to others and able to key into feelings, both his own and someone else's. He can translate ideas into reality, like a painter or musician who dreams up an idea and brings it to life, or a writer who takes obscure ideas and expresses them in a coherent manner. There are also important health matters that appear on or near this part of the hand (see Chapter 12).

## The Ulna Mounts

## Apollo

If well developed, this mount indicates charm, good manners, creativity, a liking for children and animals, sports, arts and hobbies. This person will have great style. If overdeveloped he might be greedy, extravagant and vain, and he could be a gambler.

### Mercury

This mount is concerned with self-expression, communications, business, machinery, money, literary and scientific matters, health and relationships. If well developed, he will be comfortable with computers and other modern machinery. If overdeveloped, the subject could be a cunning confidence trickster. If underdeveloped, he may be painfully shy, unable to express himself, with no business acumen.

### Luna (Fig. 2.13)

This relates to the unconscious, the imagination, creativity, travel, and also a love of the sea and a need for freedom. If well developed, there could be a liking for gentle outdoor sports and pursuits such as fishing. A high mount of Luna is supposed to show linguistic ability, but we feel a love of travel is just as likely.

### Pluto (Fig. 1.1)

If this mount is developed the subject is extremely restless and he needs to get away from his normal environment from time to time. He has a talent for translating theoretical ideas into practice.

### Upper Mars (Fig. 2.13)

Tenacity, courage, aggression. If fairly full and thick at the percussion edge, the subject will be able to cope with a crisis. He is not easily surprised or flabbergasted and he can stand up for himself. If this is exceptionally prominent, high, full and stands upwards and outwards from the hand at the percussion edge, the subject may be argumentative, possibly in extreme cases with a violent temper.

A mount that curves outwards at the percussion on both Mars and Luna is a sign of creativity.(a) This person would find his own method of doing things. If the edge is

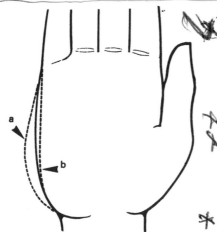

Figure 2.13  A bulge at the Percussion edge

straight, the subject can interpret ideas. (b) The first person would be able to work out original ideas whereas the second could carry them out. If the head line goes into the upper Mars area, the subject is a very convincing salesman.

### Plain of Mars

This is the center of the hand. It has no specific character of its own but it is the area where the lines cross, influence and activate one another.

## The Elements

It has become common for palmists to use the medieval categories of the four Elements, which are Earth, Air, Fire and Water, as a means of describing certain types and shapes of hands.

These classifications may or may not connect with the astrological sign of the person but they do give a clue as to their nature. This is how it works in practice.

## The Earth Hand (Fig 2.14)

- Square palm, short fingers
- Down to earth, warm-hearted
- Prefers a regular routine
- Dependable

This is much the same as the square hand, although there can be a few slight variations on the theme. The palm is square; the fingers short to medium in length and either smooth or slightly knotted at the second joint. The nails are square shaped, although there are variations. The lines on the hand are either straight or slightly bent but not deeply curved in any direction. The hand feels firm, dry and warm.

Figure 2.14

The Earth subject is good with his hands and, if the third phalanx of each finger is thick, he likes money. He enjoys good food and drink and may be quite fussy about these things. He loves his family and will put up with a lot from them, because he considers that aggravation is better than loneliness. However, what he most wants is a regular routine kind of life at home, at work and in bed.

## The Air Hand (Fig. 2.15)

- Wide or triangular palm with longish fingers
- Eccentric, artistic, understanding, cool and detached; shows love by sharing

Figure 2.15

This hand has a distinctive shape with fingers that are set in a sloping fashion. The Jupiter finger is set high and the other three fingers (Saturn, Apollo and Mercury) are each set a little lower, with Mercury being rather low set. The palm has a characteristically triangular shape, due to the fact that the percussion is very slanted, coming sharply in from a prominent bone in the area of the attachment lines to the rather narrow area above the wrist. If the fingers are smooth, fat and blunt, the person will be selfish. The fingernails are often hard and, in the case of a female subject, sharpened to a point.

The knotted Air hand belongs to an intellectual subject who uses his mind more than his body, while the smoother or spiky variety of finger on this type of hand shows an athletic, sporty type of person who cannot sit still for long. This person must have plenty to do both inside and outside of the home. Often talented, especially where music, drama and movement are concerned, they seem to waste their talents and end up achieving little. These clever people can live well, often due to the efforts of others, but their good nature and pleasant manners give them the ability to get away with things in situations where others would be swiftly dumped.

## The Fire Hand (Fig. 2.16)

- Long palm and short, straight fingers
- Practical, sociable, restless, and assertive

This hand has a long rectangular palm and rather short fingers. The skin is smooth and the fingers are often knotted. The fingernails are long and possibly a little narrow. The hands are attractive to look at and they are rarely still. The lines on the hand are straight or mildly curved. In a more tenacious personality the nails

Figure 2.16

will be quite hard, while in a more flexible and less determined person they will be soft and flaky.

The Fire person has tremendous enthusiasm for life and also great courage. He is easily bored and very restless. He needs large-scale projects in order to sop up his energies, especially if the base of the hand is fairly full. He may be creative and artistic, especially if the lines on the hand are curved. Indeed, he could have considerable success in a creative field once he has overcome any lack of self-esteem that may be left over from childhood.

## The Water Hand (Fig. 2.17)

- Long palm, long fingers
- Self-contained, emotional, sensitive, creative, complex

This hand has a long palm and long fingers and all the lines are curved. The shape of the hand may be medium to narrow. This person is sensitive to atmospheres and also to outside stimulation. He may need to be away from others from time to time in order to rid himself of their emotions and their demands. Often artistic and musical, this type needs a

Figure 2.17

creative outlet and an opportunity for self-expression. He may not have a normal job, preferring to live his life to his own standards and satisfaction than according to a set of rules laid down by others. He may profess to values that are above or removed from daily life and he may not wish to compromise his ideals. Oddly enough, this doesn't prevent him from having a high income because water people are often extremely shrewd and careful (and also often lucky!) with money.

Water types have a great sense of humor and a fascinating store of off-beat knowledge. Their extreme self-absorption and inability to take on anything that will tax their patience or deflect them from their chosen lifestyle makes them difficult to live with. However, as friends, they are kindness itself and great company.

# CHAPTER THREE

# FINGERS AND PHALANGES

## Length of Fingers

Average fingers are about three-quarters to seven-eighths the length of the palm, short fingers are less than three-quarters and long fingers are the same length or longer than the palm. Long-fingered people have patience with detail but find it hard to motivate themselves and they find large-scale projects off-putting. Short-fingered people are starters, not runners. They have initiative and can conceive grand plans but they are quickly bored with detailed work and daily chores. It is interesting to note that people who have somewhat stubby fat fingers often love music but they may not have the patience to master an instrument. Long-fingered people have talent and patience but often lack the energy and initiative to cash in on their gifts. On a normal hand the Saturn (medius or middle) finger is the longest, with either the Jupiter (index) or Apollo (ring) finger coming next, and the Mercury (little) finger either being the shortest or the same length as the Jupiter finger.

## Through Thick and Thin

Thick-fingered people do not like to waste time. They often jump straight into a situation and get on with it (especially if the fingers are short). They may live or work in a mess because they prefer to be doing something purposeful rather than spend time clearing up. Their minds work quickly and they focus intuitively on a problem to produce the ideal solution. They are direct and honest, but tactless. They do not set out to hurt other people's feelings; it is just that sometimes they forget to think and lack patience with those who they consider to be fools. Thin-fingered people are more precise in their thinking. They need to take time analyzing a task and tackle it in a logical manner. They are thoughtful, diplomatic and patient.

## Knuckles

Knobbly knuckles are a feature of rather cautious people who choose to play it safe. They may moan and groan on occasion about their situation but will put up with the status quo rather than face up to making a change.

## Knots of Mental Order

Knotty first knuckles (near the fingertips) suggest a methodical mind that is good at logic or research, but they are not usually given to flashes of intuition.

## Knots of Material Order

Knots on the second knuckles (middle of the fingers) suggest a person who works in an orderly fashion that is logical but not as hidebound as the subject with knots on both sets of knuckles.

## How the Fingers are Set (Figs. 3.1 and 3.2)

The junction where the fingers join the hands varies from one person to another. We refer to this base level of the fingers as the setting. Some people have a gentle curve where their fingers join their palm, others have a straight line. The setting of the fingers may disguise their true length by making one finger appear shorter than the others. The easiest way to measure the *exact* length of each finger is to take a bit of ribbon and a felt-tipped pen and mark off each finger against the ribbon.

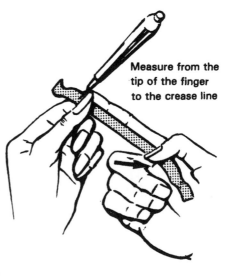

**Measure from the tip of the finger to the crease line**

Figure 3.1 Measuring fingers

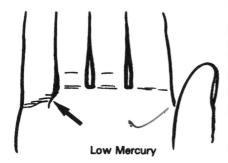

Fingers that are set in line suggest a rigid, ambitious personality; a gentle curve denotes a balanced personality; and a very sharp V formation belongs to someone who has a giant sense of inadequacy.

**Low Mercury**

## The Jupiter Finger

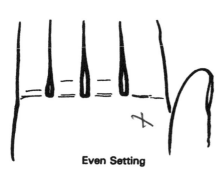

**Even Setting**

### Long Jupiter finger
These people like to have their own way and need to stamp their personality on their surroundings. They are unable to sacrifice their independence for the sake of others. They tend to have strong, highly personal, religious or philosophical views. They are ambitious, hard to dominate, influence or change. The ego is well developed and the personality may run from sociable and well adjusted to pompous, self-important or just plain selfish. They are very interested in money because of the power and the security it represents and they will go all out to find and keep it. They may hoard it or spend it, depending on other factors on the hand, but they must have access to it.

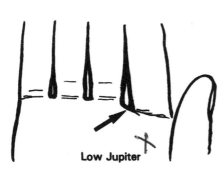

**Low Jupiter**

Figure 3.2   Settings

### Short Jupiter finger
People with short Jupiter fingers lack a sense of conviction. Lacking confidence in themselves, they may not have a clear idea of their direction in life, or even of their own identity. They tend to measure

themselves by other people's standards and can lose heart when criticized. They need reassurance from others. These people can be fairly easily manipulated and are willing to sacrifice their own desires for
the needs of others. Often very loving and caring, they must make
sure that they do leave time for themselves to pursue their own
interests. It would help them if they could learn to rely on their
own judgement.

Sometimes a long Apollo finger can make the Jupiter finger *seem*
short, also a low-set Jupiter will look shorter than it is. If the Jupiter
finger is shorter than the Apollo finger, the subject may have a personality which is perfectly well adjusted but he will be more interested in expressing his creativity than in making or keeping a lot of
money.

### High-set Jupiter finger

This indicates self-confidence and ambition. If the finger is also long
and carries a whorl pattern on the fingerprint, there is very little
which would stop this person from achieving his aims in life.

### Level-set Jupiter finger

This shows a balanced attitude. This subject is neither over-
ambitious, egotistical, timid nor retiring. He is helpful and understanding up to a point; he likes to make his own decisions but will
cooperate and discuss these where appropriate.

### Low-set Jupiter finger

This setting represents quite a problem as the subject is very unsure
of himself. He lacks the courage or ability to stand up for himself. He
may be extremely shy, especially if there is an arch formation on the
pad of the finger. He prefers others to make decisions, fits in with
other people's plans and does not like to speak out even on his own
behalf. There could be a tendency to self-sacrifice or martyrdom.

### Discrepancies between the hands

This shows that the person has changed himself due to circumstances. If the minor hand has the longer Jupiter finger, then the subject's personality has been squashed by the demands of other people.
If the dominant hand has the longer Jupiter finger—which is a much
more common feature—then the subject has learned how to express

his personality and to exert his will power. He has made himself fight
for his rightful share of a place in the sun.

## The Saturn Finger

This finger is associated with the everyday practicalities and problems
of earning a living. It is usually the longest finger on the hand and
may sit squarely on a line with Jupiter, Apollo or both. Most people
have square or slightly conic finger ends and nails on the Saturn
finger. It is associated with farming, property, land and investments,
also the ability to study, scientific aptitudes and the gloomier aspects
of religious or philosophical thought. It marks the balance between
the radial and ulna sides of the hand and shows how the conscious
and unconscious sides of the subject's nature blend together.

### Long Saturn finger

This is often found in serious people who can study hard and concentrate on a project, and this is especially so if the head line travels
straight across the hand aiming directly for the percussion edge. If
the finger is exceptionally long, the subject will be pessimistic, easily
downhearted, even morbid. If a number of fine lines suddenly
appear on the mount of Saturn, the subject would be going through
a period of depression. A reasonably long Saturn finger endows
good organizational skills and an instinctive understanding of economics. This person will be materialistic, especially if the third phalange is full and fat. If the hands are either square or claw-like, this
subject will never take any kind of risk. The combination of long
Jupiter and Saturn fingers point to strong religious views with a
blinkered and inflexible attitude, especially if the fingers are stiff and
unbending.

A reasonably long Saturn finger shows that the subject is interested in emotional and financial stability. There will be a sensible attitude
toward saving. This person takes out a mortgage and then takes good
care of the property. There will be a love of the countryside and an
interest in ecology and the preservation and protection of our planet.

### Short Saturn finger

This person is venturesome, so he will take a chance on life and in
business. If the Apollo finger is rather long and stays close to the

Saturn finger, then there will be an instinct for gambling and risk tak-ing. If the Jupiter finger is the closest in length and proximity to Saturn, then the subject will be egotistical and he may not really con-sider the possibility of failure. Popular and successful show-business personalities tend to have Saturn, Apollo and even Jupiter fingers all of more or less the same length. Those who have short Saturn fingers may be untidy and disorganized or compulsive gamblers, but if the Saturn finger is not too short, they will display great zest for life and the ability to back a hunch and win. They are not so good at con-serving their winnings and need a partner with longer Saturn fingers to help them save sensibly.

### Setting and the Saturn finger

This finger is nearly always set either on a level with the adjoining fingers or perhaps a little higher. In the rare case of a subject with a low-set Saturn finger, he would be unable to cope with daily life and would lack balance between the conscious and unconscious mind leading to very inconsistent behavior. He could be aggressive, violent and even psychotic.

## The Apollo Finger

This finger is associated with the more enjoyable aspects of life such as creativity and the inclination to take chances in life that may range from slight risks to out and out gambles. The Apollo finger deals with the fatalistic dreamy side of life and will indicate success of a glam-orous kind if there are other harder features showing on the hand, such as a longish Saturn finger and a strongly formed head line and/or fate line. It is also connected with the home and family and the love of children.

### Long Apollo finger

Be careful when determining the actual length of the fingers here as they may be disguised by the setting on the hand.

These subjects have pleasant manners and a nice appearance. They like good clothes and need attractive surroundings. They are broad-minded, generous, less likely to live by the book than others and less inhibited than most. They may not be quite of this world, and per-haps too ready to bet their week's wages at the racing track, but they are fun. Self-expression is more important than financial gain. This subject may be artistic and musical, especially if the first phalange splays outwards, or a clever craftsman if the first phalange carries a droplet. The natural dreaminess may not be too noticeable to others if all the fingers are fairly short, the thumb is strong and the head line not too curved. These people are fond of children and enjoy home life, as long as the atmosphere at home is pleasant and easygoing. They will make sacrifices for the family and would always prefer to live in harmony rather than fight for their rights. They can be quite ambitious with regard to their creative interests, especially if the Jupiter finger leans toward Saturn.

### Short Apollo finger

This subject is ambitious, self-motivated and not about to make sacrifices on behalf of others. He is capable and practical, and not usually given to fits of dreamy irresponsibility. If the head line and life line are "tied" where they start on the hands, he will seek security, and will want guarantees wherever possible. He may either be somewhat narrow-minded or will just see things his own way. If there is a long Mercury finger, this person could be a good public speaker but rather a misery in private life. He is responsible, reliable and decent, if rather boring. He would not be an inventive lover.

### Setting and the Apollo finger

When set in line with Saturn, there is an air of confidence and optimism, and any creativity will be of a practical nature. If it is set significantly lower than the Saturn finger, the subject is not so imaginative and may despise anything which does not have a practical use.

## The Mercury Finger

This finger really is the most difficult to understand as it is on the ulna (instinctive) side of the hand but it is concerned with how people express themselves. It shows how they go about getting what they need by day-to-day cooperation and interaction with others.

This finger shows how they communicate—whether they are fluent talkers, good writers or have the ability to sort out ideas and images logically. It can show truthfulness or otherwise. Does a person need the excitement and challenge of a career in sales or finance or does he just prefer to plod along in a steadily familiar job? Even sexual communication is shown on this finger.

### Long Mercury finger

Setting can make this finger look short when in fact it is not. The long Mercury finger belongs to a subject who can express himself well. If the Saturn finger is also long and he has a long straight head line with a fairly firmly marked fate line he will have a scientific mind. The mind is imaginative and creative if the Apollo finger is long, there is a slope to the head line and a well-defined Apollo line. These people have broad minds as they want to know what is going on in the world. They are sociable and they learn from chatting to others. They make good students and teachers as they cannot resist the opportunity of communicating and spreading knowledge. They may be wordy, verbose and possibly boring when on their favorite soap box, unless there is a little loop of humor on the hand between the mounts of Mercury and Apollo. They are drawn towards intelligent and interesting people. Anybody who needs to influence others, be it politically, in business, in the fields of science, education, literature or art, will need at least a reasonably long Mercury with a long first and second phalange. This is also true for negotiators and business people who need to confer with or organize others.

A slight curve in this finger shows both business sense and a sensible attitude to money. This subject has a fairly firm attitude with the ability to stick to his guns and finish what he starts. Too great a curve indicates obstinacy.

There is something to be gleaned from the Mercury finger about the subject's attitude to sex. If the finger is long and straight he might pursue those who he fancies, if curved, then more of a family man and rather choosy about whom he marries. A little step on the inside of the third phalange also shows sexuality.

### Short Mercury finger

This is an indication of intense shyness. This subject will take a long time to gain the confidence and maturity to go after who he fancies, and this is especially so if the moons are wholly or partly missing from all the fingernails. He cringes at the thought of having to speak in public or of being in the limelight. This does not mean that the subject has a poor opinion of himself—on the contrary, he may have quite a large ego but he just hates to be exposed. He is easily embarrassed and soon becomes tongue-tied. He prefers to lead a quiet life and to be a backroom boy rather than a front runner.

One kind of subject with a short Mercury finger would be the type of little man who attaches himself to a large and overpowering woman. This man may in fact be quite obstinate and awkward to live with—after all, he is afraid of life and narrow-minded. He does not read much and he is a creature of habit and safety. He lives a rich life at second hand through his lady wife! He may have strange secret sexual desires but would run a mile if he had to carry them through.

### Exceptionally short Mercury finger

This shows some kind of sexual peculiarity. This person may have a severe lack of confidence, due to being unusually tall, short, fat, thin etc. The subject could have a nice appearance but *feel* himself to be unattractive. He finds it difficult to express himself sexually and hard to keep the attention of the opposite sex. This is sometimes a sign of mental handicap.

### Setting and the Mercury finger

The Mercury finger can be set in line with the other fingers or lower. If set in line, the personality will be fairly outgoing and business-like. If low set, he will have talent but this will be expressed in private through work and study at home. These people have a creative imagination and may be writers or artists. They dream a little too much, especially if there is a very sloping head line. There could be a tendency toward self-deception and daydreaming if the subjects have a long sloping head line and a high mount of Neptune, but this may only be a necessary part of their creative mentality.

There may be a somewhat amoral attitude to money and possessions or a different way of looking at these things if this finger is extremely bent and twisted. Sometimes the person is good to his family members but not to outsiders.

## Inclining or Laterally Curving Fingers (Fig. 3.3)

The way fingers curve and lean toward each other is important. Ask your subject to hold his hands upright, or better still, take a print of his hand. Look at the fingertips to see if they lean naturally toward

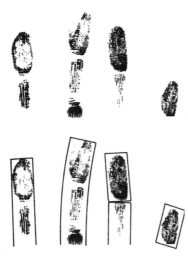

Figure 3.3    Inclination

any of the other fingers, as this will show where the flow of energy is inhibited and has become dependent upon the energy of the finger it leans upon. This leaning must be natural and not due to disease or malformation. If one finger is slightly tucked behind another, think of the energies attached to those fingers and apply a little logic. For instance, when the Apollo finger is tucked under the Saturn finger on the dominant hand, the subject's creativity is stifled by a regimented routine or limiting circumstances. If the top phalange is bent, the mental faculties will be inhibited, making the subject a slow thinker or he may have a depressive personality.

### Jupiter finger curved towards the thumb

This person has a materialistic outlook on life and a dynamic, purposeful personality. His independent nature also needs personal freedom, especially if there is a fair-sized gap between the Jupiter and Saturn fingers. However, he can be indecisive in matters of love.

### Jupiter finger curved towards Saturn

Self-assertion, an attitude of a positive, persistent working towards aims and intentions. This subject sets out to get what he wants. He is inclined to be emotionally secretive and finds it hard to unwind and reveal his true self. He may *appear* to be open and chatty and full of interesting anecdotes but will not say anything that is personally revealing.

### Saturn finger curved towards Jupiter

A serious type of person, who is emotionally rather inhibited. He may look outwards for happiness by seeking recognition in sports or some other kind of achievement. He is restless and ambitious.

**Jupiter and Saturn both curved towards Apollo and Mercury**
A need for inner understanding. If the life line curves around the lower part of the mount of Venus, this person needs inner understanding more than a great career.

**Saturn curved towards Apollo**
This person is pressurized by family, domestic demands and duties that may conflict with his career. He searches for self-expression, a feeling of achievement and job satisfaction, not necessarily for more money.

There is an old wives' tale that if the top phalanges of Saturn fingers on both hands bend sideways toward Apollo, the subject will write for a living and that seems to be true.

**Saturn and Apollo curving away from each other**
When these two fingers fall away from each other, the person has a rebellious and non-conformist nature.

**Apollo curved toward Saturn**
These people get no pleasure from domestic responsibilities and they find housework boring. They prefer to be professional people. Emotional, intuitive, intellectual and rational, they may have an inferiority complex. If the top phalange bends toward Saturn, this may give a mediumistic quality.

**Mercury finger curved toward Apollo**
This person can help people by talking, listening and consoling those who are unhappy. If the curve is extreme, they are shrewd in business and good salesmen, as long as they believe in their product. They have an optimistic nature but may be rather defensive. They make up their own minds.

**Mercury finger curving outwards**
These subjects need someone reliable to give them backing and encouragement. They prefer to blend in with the environment and not to press their own opinion on others.

## Phalanges

Each finger is divided into three phalanges. The first phalange shows how we think, the second shows how we apply that thinking and the third shows our basic needs.

Thick phalanges show a coarse side to the nature whilst slender phalanges show refinement and delicacy. At the same time, one must bear in mind that thicker phalanges show energy and enterprise while the slim phalanges show a weaker, more nervous nature.

## The First Phalange

This includes the fingertips and fingernails. Fingertips, like toes, are the extremities of the body and they are the first to shrivel and die if the body is under severe attack through illness or frostbite. They give the palmist the first impression of the subject and his nature. They show how the subject views the world about him and the influence he has upon it.

### Long first phalanges

Intuitive, studious and orderly. The outlook is philosophical and religious rather than materialistic. These people delight in mental activities such as debating, reading and crossword puzzles, they enjoy new ideas and they can be very entertaining.

### Short first phalanges

Materialistic, possibly practical and suspicious. These subjects only understand tangibles and have little sense of faith or inspiration. They are mentally lazy and not inclined to study or grasp new concepts.

## Fingertips

### Rounded tips (Fig 3.4)

These people do not like friction. They seek beauty, truth and they can be too trusting. They are open-minded, creative; they make clever, shrewd, fairly cautious and honest decisions.

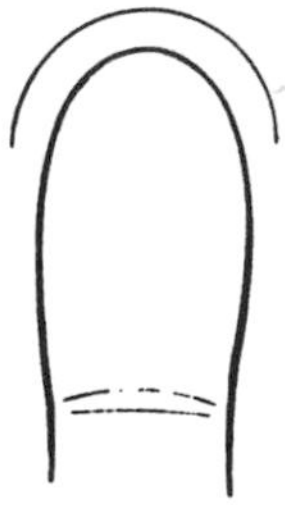

Figure 3.4 Rounded fingertip

### Pointed tips (Fig. 3.5)

These people can have pin-sharp minds and quick intellects. They go to the heart of a matter, sum up the situation quickly but they cannot see the overall picture. They react instinctively to people and they form immediate likes and dislikes, and once these opinions are formed they are uncompromising. This makes it difficult for them to act diplomatically or to see behind someone else's outer manner or to find excuses for the behavior or attitude of those they do not take to. They have good organizational and delegation skills but cannot cope with too many details.

Figure 3.5
Pointed fingertip

Very pointed fingertips belong to the beautiful dreamer. These people are cautious, discreet and they have a mental ideal of the kind of life which would best suit themselves. They are frequently very good looking, they pay attention to their appearance and are personally fussy. They can be a source of inspiration to others but lack the energy to do much for themselves and they certainly will not set out to do anything for others.

### Spatulate tips (Fig. 3.6)

These fingertips belong to outgoing, independent people who have restless minds. They can see the larger picture and bring component parts together, therefore they can be scientists and lawyers, in addition to successful performers and sportsmen. They like to bring the fruits of their hands and brains together, so they may also be inventive craftsmen and engineers.

Figure 3.6
Spatulate fingertip

### Square tips (Fig. 3.7)

These are down-to-earth people who have a blunt manner and a slow mind. They are conformists, so they can be dogmatic and conservative. They like to see justice done. If the phalanges are long, they make good lawyers, bankers, clerks and counselors. They work well with documents and they can cope with details.

Figure 3.7   Square fingertip

## Side View of the First Phalange

### Tapering tips (Fig. 3.8)

These people put their minds to good use, but they lack physical stamina. They are imaginative, affectionate and spiritual rather than materialistic in outlook.

Figure 3.8
Tapering fingertip

### Coarse heavy tips (Fig. 3.9)

These people are down-to-earth, materialistic, sensual, self-indulgent and occasionally coarse in behavior. If the phalange is short, they could be unimaginative plodders, while if long, quite sharp in business, capable and not likely to be beaten in an argument.

Figure 3.9
Coarse fingertip

### Bulgy tip, droplets (Fig. 3.10)

These people are more refined than the coarse-tipped types and they have a highly developed sense of touch. Amazingly dexterous, they rarely drop anything. They are sensitive, intellectual and they have creative gifts. They have a well-developed sense of touch which is useful when dressmaking, gardening, creating a sculpture or playing a musical instrument. This is even more so if there is a prominent droplet on Apollo. Their natures can be rather intense and one must look at the head line to see if it slopes to Luna, indicating a sensitive mind.

Figure 3.10
Bulgy fingertip

## Fingerprints

Fingerprints are formed before birth and they are an unchanging inherited characteristic. Each person's prints are said to be unique, although police records have shown that there are some who share at least one or two identical prints. Fingerprint patterns must be read bearing in mind the shape of the hand, the fingers, thumb and the head line. The other parts of the hand will show how the subject deals with the inborn characteristics that are locked up in the prints. Ideally each print pattern should be in, or just below, the center of the first phalange of each finger. It is possible to find hands that carry only one type of print—usually loops or whorls, but most people have a mixture of prints.

### The arch (Fig. 3.11)

Figure 3.11
The arch fingerprint

This is shaped like a humpbacked bridge and it deflects energy back down the finger. It represents the simplest type of personality, which is practical, shy and rather ordinary. If there are many suppression lines below the arch, this will add tension and neurosis to the personality. Arches do not bestow an easy life and everything has to be worked for. The personality is withdrawn, inward looking, secretive and self-defensive. There may have been unhappiness and unpleasant events early in life. Subjects who have more than just a couple of arches need to be encouraged to be a little more trusting, more outgoing and to think more positively about their problems. Although very unsure of themselves, if they do become fired by enthusiasm, either for a project or a person, they can go overboard and bore everyone else to death with their obsession. They are not intellectual but that does not mean that they cannot appreciate the finer things in life.

Figure 3.12
The composite whorl fingerprint

### The composite whorl or double loop (Fig. 3.12)

This looks like a side view of two hands that are interlocked. The energy of the whorl goes into the center where the two forces meet. This leads to duality, indecision, the ability to see both sides of an argument or the possibilities of two courses of action. We have noticed that psychic people seem to have this formation on their thumbs or their Jupiter fingers. A double loop on the Mercury finger may show bisexuality.

### The whorl (Fig. 3.13)

This looks like a whirlpool with the energy running smoothly into the center. These people are self-centered and orientated towards the inner realms of thought, individualism and independence. They have strong reserves of inner strength and determination that cause them to set their own standards and carve their own path through life. If there are many whorls on the fingers (and especially on the Jupiter finger) this subject will be hard working and very successful, and doors will open for him. Cool, calculating and emotionally controlled, this is the anti-hero type. This person would do well in the armed services where his highly tuned and carefully focused intellect would take him to the top. Although rarely emotionally vulnerable, such people may wonder why they do not get too much out of relationships. They need a compliant marriage partner who is either content to remain in the background or who has a separate career and interests.

Figure 3.13
The whorl fingerprint

### A whorl on Jupiter

This person has a narrow focus on life and is unable to see other points of view or understand other people's way of life. He is probably not that interested in other people anyway. He pays great attention to his career and focuses on its direction without being distracted by potentially competing issues.

### A whorl on Saturn

This person may be too serious, and he may even be a depressive, lonely character. He is self-disciplined and successful in a highly original way, and he can be ambitious and obstinate with an air of superiority, self-importance and a touch-me-not attitude. The marriage partner will be chosen for suitability.

### A whorl on Apollo

This denotes artistic ability and the kind of person who sets the emotional standards. He considers himself entitled to dictate his partner's behavior and feelings. Personal tastes are set early in life and he finds it hard to change them.

### A whorl on Mercury

This suggests teaching ability and a person who wants to expand mental horizons, research and to reach for answers. Journalists, broadcasters, seekers after truth share this mark. This subject is determined, successful but shy and unsure of himself emotionally.

### The loop (Fig. 3.14)

This is the most commonly found pattern in which the energy is deflected to one side or the other. The loops usually enter the fingers from the ulna side with the occasional radial loop on the Jupiter finger. This person is friendly, adaptable and responsive to people. He is a good team worker who needs variety both in working and social life. The mind is lively, elastic, quick and humorous. He is so interested in all that is going on around him that he may miss out on success by spending too much time on unnecessary

Figure 3.14
The loop fingerprint

projects, or he may waste time and energy on other people and their problems. This subject gets bored quickly and has to make an effort to concentrate on each task and finish what he starts. Being rather wary of committing himself, he leaves the door open so that he can make a quick getaway from a situation which threatens to become too onerous.

### The tented arch (Fig. 3.15)

The energy flows straight up the finger, glancing neither to the left nor the right. A subject with a few of these would be straightforward and straight-faced. He could be idealistic, creative or sporting and obsessive about personal projects. It is hard for him to cope with changing times, and unexpected events might cause him to become temporarily unhinged, especially if there are suppression lines. This subject is highly strung, over-enthusiastic and sensitive to criticism but could be very successful for all that.

Figure 3.15
The tented arch fingerprint

### The peacock's eye (Fig. 3.16)

Figure 3.16
The peacock's eye fingerprint

This formation rarely appears on more than one or two fingers, and not necessarily on both hands. It combines the intensity of the whorl with the flexibility of the loop and it indicates talent. The finger where it appears will show where the talent lies. For instance, if on Mercury, then communication ability (writing and speaking) will be present. It is also supposed to have magical life-saving qualities when there.

## Some Problem Prints

### (Fig. 3.17a)
Arch with suppression ridges that show a defeatist mentality, a person who holds himself back from a challenge and who is not good at coping with problems.

### (Fig. 3.17b)
A string-of-pearls formation indicating frustration and resentment.

Figure 3.17

***(Fig. 3.18)***
A whorl that is just about visible. This print was taken from an elderly lady whose sight is failing and is similar to the palm pattern of the insomniac.

Figure 3.18

***(Fig. 3.19a)***
The suppression lines are displaced to one side showing the push-pull effect on the character, making him want to be assertive and tough, but more likely to be bombastic. This is a displaced arch pattern.

***(Fig. 3.19b)***
The core is a whorl which shows a know-it-all attitude, but the slightly off-center placement indicates angry outbursts rather than quiet self-confidence.

**Centre line**

***(Fig. 3.19c)***
The lines pressing down on the whorl add an almost arched look to the formation implying a lack of self-confidence under the blustering outer manner. This person is a bully.

Figure 3.19

***(Fig. 3.20)***
Warts signify long-term stress, in this case mental anguish.

## Top, middle and lower phalanges

Figure 3.20

- Top relates to mental, spiritual and emotional needs.
- Middle relates to application of ideas, practicalities and putting things into action.
- Lower relates to material matters and physical needs.

## Long phalanges

*Jupiter*
- Top: Emotional, sensitive, religious.
- Middle: Practical worker, determined, ambitious.
- Bottom: Worldly, inflexible, self-indulgent, a flashy dresser, has an urge to rule.

*Saturn*
- Top: Loner, withdrawn personality, prudent, suicidal.
- Middle: Lone worker, cautious, money minded, interested in agricultural pursuits.
- Bottom: Hoards, mistrusts, greedy.

*Apollo*
- Top: Mental stress in creative people.
- Middle: Likes beauty, musical, good designer, idealist.
- Bottom: Likes luxury, makes money from entertainment or art. Successful

*Mercury*
- Top: Abstract thinker with unusual mind, studious, literary.
- Middle: Rational, good business person.
- Bottom: Restless, fraudulent trickster, skilled but cunning.

## Short Phalanges

*Jupiter*
- Top: Materialistic, shallow, untrusting.
- Middle: Lacks ambition, lazy.
- Bottom: Poor self-image, hides away from life, prefers to be alone with own interests.

*Saturn*
- Top: Resignation, contentment, calm, steady personality.
- Middle: Insignificant, ignorant, time-waster.
- Bottom: Economical, frugal, mean.

*Apollo*
- Top: Lacks artistic feelings and ideas.
- Middle: No inspiration or potential, may be a failure.
- Bottom: Lack of skills in art, crafts and mechanics.

*Mercury*
- Top: Lack of alertness, mentally lazy, dull.
- Middle: Lack of initiative.
- Bottom: Simplicity, gullibility.

## Nails and Temperament

The fingernails are an excellent indicator of a person's current state of health, but there is also some information about personality which can be gleaned from them. The following descriptions presuppose that the subjects are not suffering from any physical or mental illness.

Figure 3.21

### Wide short nails (Fig. 3.21)
High energy level, the energy is quickly reflected back down the finger. These subjects have a quick temper but are equally quick to forgive. Their reactions are fast, they are quick witted and they can be sharp tongued. Sexually and emotionally aggressive, they are prone to jealousy and possessiveness. They like to argue the point and can be sharply critical. They are not interested in the feelings of others, especially when in a competitive situation. If *they* are proved wrong, they sulk and do not take criticism kindly. If the nails are very small the outlook is narrow and bigoted (especially if the head and heart lines are close together).

Figure 3.22

### Wide long nails (Fig. 3.22)
The energy takes longer to be reflected—this shows caution, sense, reserve. These people can be nervy but have a frank and kindly nature. They are sympathetic, emotional and reliable in affections. They prefer practical jobs and creative pursuits to sports. They are deep thinkers but they lack vigor and competitive spirit.

### Wide rounded nails (Fig. 3.23)
The nail is as wide as it is long but rounded at the moons. The energy flows smoothly around it. These placid-natured people prefer discussion to argument.

Figure 3.23

They may worry but rarely feel tense or angry, and they prefer not to be spiteful or hurtful. The flow of energy reflects their gentle and sensible manner. They can become dreamy and detached from reality if they have a long flowing head line.

### Short spatulate nails (Fig. 3.24)

Figure 3.24

The energy flows quickly around the nail. There are two distinct types of nature that go with this nail. One is placid and lacking in vitality, and the person may endure some long drawn-out kind of illness. If he becomes angry, this is probably due to underlying illness. The hands would be small and soft.

If the hands are firm, full of hard-packed fat with deeply-embedded white or blueish nails, there can be an explosive temperament. This person is highly ambitious but he also wants to be liked and admired by others. Bigoted, moody, extremely unpleasant at times, although charming when wanting something, this type should take up some extremely competitive sport in order to burn off the excess of tension and competitiveness. If the nails lie on top of the fingers as if they were not securely attached, the subject will have a whining, complaining manner and will be too lazy to engage in sport.

Figure 3.25

### Long narrow nails (Fig. 3.25)

These are usually only found on women. The energy flows quickly past the nail on either side. A lot of flesh showing on either side of the nail shows selfishness. These people can be superficially charming and even a little babyish at times, but make no mistake, they are ambitious, possessive and materialistic. They like the good things of life without expending too much effort to get them. The narrower the nail, the more touchy they are. If the nails grow long, the more mercenary they are, especially if there are also whorls on Jupiter and Apollo.

### Curved claw-like nails

These are long and narrow nails, but they curve in a claw-like fashion. They imply greed and possessiveness. If anyone tries to get in this person's way, there is every likelihood of their talons being used to clear their path once again.

There are some racial indications here. If the subject is black, brown or Jewish, the curved nails are a natural feature and therefore have no special meaning.

### Very small nails

These indicate poor resistance to disease but also a weak, self-centered nature. There could be a foul temper. This person is critical, sarcastic and hurtful.

# CHAPTER FOUR

# THE THUMB

## The Overall Picture

If the thumb is large and strong, the subject is courageous, vigorous, extroverted and strong-willed. If it is small and weak, the subject is ailing, introverted and lacks courage.

The thumb is on the radial side of the hand so it affects the way one deals with life in practical terms. It shows the measure of strength, will power, the desire for challenge or need for a quiet life, plus the ability to cope. It therefore modifies the whole hand.

A newly born baby holds its thumb close to the fingers. At about two to three months, the baby begins to reach out and touch objects around it. By then it is stronger, more accustomed to its surroundings and beginning to look outwards at the world around it. When it feels miserable it may suck its thumb for comfort.

A thumb that is tucked into the hand is a sure sign of insecurity, depression, lack of confidence and helplessness, especially if the fingers are held tightly together and curled around the thumb. When someone is near to death, as the life force ebbs away, the thumb will drop into the hand. A thumb that is held naturally is a sure sign of confidence and strength.

The thumb is such a strong indicator of the force of character and behavior that some eastern palmists give an entire reading from it. Examine the thumb to see whether your subject has initiative and driving force and how this is used.

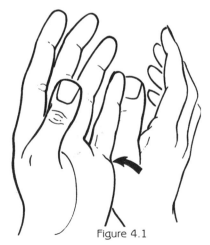

### Thumb length (Fig. 4.1)

A quick method of determining the length is to place the knuckle at the bottom of the thumb in the hollow which lies just below

Figure 4.1

the Mercury finger (the angle of dexterity). The thumb and Mercury finger should be near enough the same length.

### Length (Fig. 4.2a)

Alternatively, the thumb, when placed alongside the hand, should reach halfway up the third phalange of the Jupiter finger.

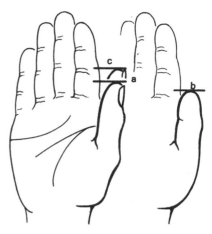

Figure 4.2

### Short thumb (Fig. 4.2b)

On an otherwise strong hand this shows weakness in the character, a tendency toward subordination. People with short thumbs do not have a strong will of their own, they are easily led and do not have much control over their own lives. If the thumb is stubby there is a lack of sensitivity; these people are aggressive, ruthless and cruel; they seek power and abuse it.

### Long thumb (Fig. 4.2c)

This denotes a rational approach to life. These people are born leaders and have natural staying power. The more refined the shape of the thumb, the more refined the person.

### High-set thumb (Fig. 4.3a)

An angle of 45 degrees or less indicates someone who has a tight rein on their emotions and a restrictive and habit-bound attitude to life with pre-judgement of situations and small-mindedness.

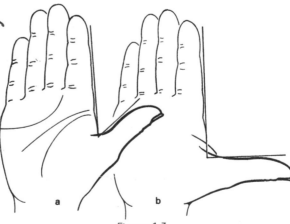

Figure 4.3

### Low-set thumb (Fig. 4.3b)

An angle of 90 degrees indicates an extrovert, adventurous and easily inspired nature, a love of new ventures. The subject is easy going, optimistic, charming and independent. An angle of about 80 degrees brings a sense of responsibility and qualities of leadership. Over 80 degrees indicates irresponsibility and foolhardiness.

### Alignment of the thumb (Fig. 4.4a)

If the thumb faces the fingers like a sergeant facing his troops, then the subject keeps himself in line. He may play the fool but he knows what he is doing.

### Alignment of the thumb (Fig. 4.4b)

Thumbnail showing on the back of the hand when the hand is at rest indicates enthusiasm, spontaneity and enjoyment of life.

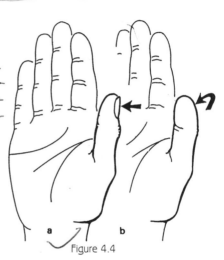

Figure 4.4

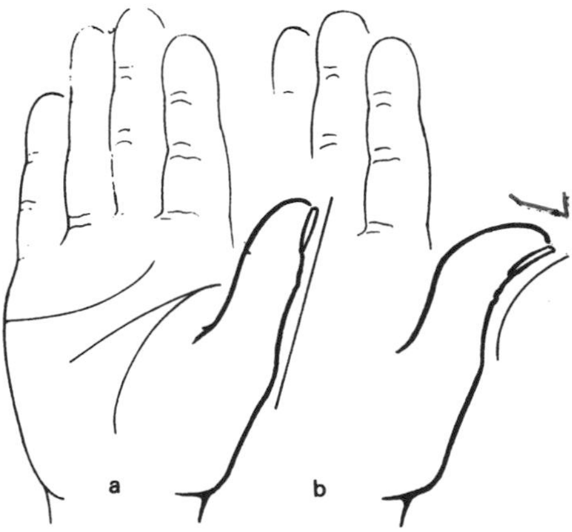

### Stiff thumb (Fig. 4.5a)

If the thumb is straight at the back, there is a strong sense of self-discipline suggesting a consistent and persistent worker with an inflexible and rigid outlook. If the top phalange bends inwards toward the fingers, this indicates narrow-mindedness, selfishness and stinginess.

### Supple thumb (Fig. 4.5b)

Known as the *spendthrift thumb*. These people go into a shop to buy an item and

Figure 4.5

end up buying something totally different. When the top phalange is flat, the person has an impulsive and generous nature. These people are entertainers who have a dramatic flair, and they can be craftsmen if they have a spatulate top phalange. If they have a weak thumb they can be a sucker for a hard luck story. These people have active minds but they like an easy life and can be lazy.

Subjects with a large thumb and a heavy top phalange will be determined, hardworking, responsible and civilized. They have the peculiarity of being very generous to themselves but not to others. They enjoy making large and important purchases both for themselves and their family but get bored by the need to give up money for mundane necessities. They love to be in the center of the action and to have full attention paid to them.

People with supple thumbs have nice manners and are often found working with the public or in sales. People with thick, stiff thumbs are blunt but honest.

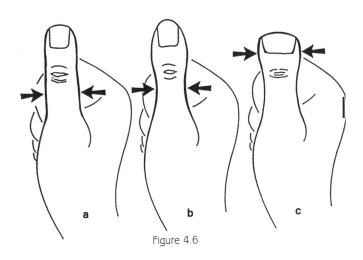

Figure 4.6

### Tubular thumb (Fig. 4.6a)
Practical by nature, these people like to buy and use things that fit and work properly.

### Wavy thumb (Fig. 4.6b)
A pleasant exterior but quite a firm nature—these people will not be put upon too much.

**Clubbed thumb (Fig. 4.6c)**

These subjects have no ability to debate or dispute, so they either back away from an argument or lose control.

## The Angle of Dexterity (Fig. 4.7)

This is also called the angle of rhythm or proficiency. If well developed, the subject is a good craftsman, he will see a job through to its end and will prefer tasks which have a physical rhythm. This may take the form of sports such as tennis or cricket, a love of music or the swinging action that a carpenter uses for sawing or planing.

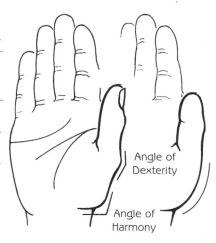

Angle of
Dexterity

Angle of
Harmony

Figure 4.7

## The Angle of Harmony (Fig. 4.7)

These people have a natural sense of the rightness of things and would like beautifully made furniture, antiques, music or attractive clothes. The greater the length between the two angles, the warmer the personality.

## Rounded edges (Fig. 4.7)

These people are easygoing and warmhearted. The energy flows quickly to the thumb, meaning a quick temper, and they are quick to warm up sexually.

## The Tip, Nail and Ball of the Thumb

The nail section of the thumb is concerned with willpower. The shape of the phalange shows how determination is used. If this is long, there is great determination that is held under control—staying power. If short, lack of willpower and self-control.

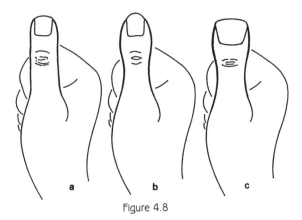

Figure 4.8

### Square tip (Fig. 4.8a)
Practical, reliable and sensible, these people can be taskmasters but like to lead the way by setting a good example.

### Conic tip (Fig. 4.8b)
A graceful approach to life. These people are quick to spot weakness in others yet spring to their defense. Easily swayed from a goal, they are impressionable, idealistic. If very wide at the joint but with a point, they will be argumentative and obstinate.

### Spatulate tip (Fig. 4.8c)
The craftsman's thumb indicates a good manual dexterity. If it is not too thick, there will be sensitivity and creativity, but it will be put to a practical use.

## Side View of Top Phalange

### Wedge shape (Fig. 4.9a)
There is a pronounced knuckle at the back end of the wedge. These subjects are stubborn and won't give an inch. Their inability to give up on a subject makes them successful lawyers, but they can be fanatics or self-absorbed pains in the neck.

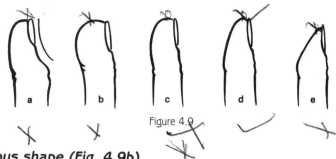

Figure 4.9

## Bulbous shape (Fig. 4.9b)

The basic appetites are near the surface, so they are passionate, obstinate and lacking in refinement. With a high mount of Venus, they will be ruthless in pursuits.

## Rounded (Fig. 4.9c)

The most commonly found shape, this symbolizes a nice balance between will and authority plus the ability to relate to the will of other people.

## Flat shape (Fig. 4.9d)

Refined, gentle but lacking energy. If the tip is conic, the subject will get his or her own way without other people really noticing what is going on, either by hinting or chiseling away until the other person gives in. An old palmistry book of ours says of this flat shape, "the possessor will yield to affection"—which probably means that they do not hold back for long before jumping into bed.

## Spoke shaved shape (Fig. 4.9e)

This shape indicates a need to be loved and appreciated. Refined, pleasant but could be too willing to give way for the sake of approval.

# Second Phalange

## Thick, straight (Fig. 4.10a)

The energy flows unimpeded up and down the thumb. This subject is straight to the point and does not like a fuss. A policeman or judge would need this kind of thumb as they deal with the facts and evidence. This subject reasons things out by what he can read or see, things must be black or white, visible, practical and tangible. He would follow conventional religious views. He may be blunt, tactless and rude, because he cannot see beneath the surface, but he is also truthful and trustworthy.

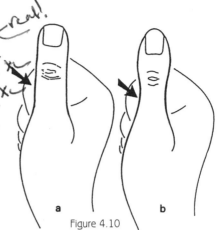

a    b

Figure 4.10

## Length of the first and second phalanges

The two phalanges should be approximately the same length. If the second phalange is longer than the first it reveals one who may spend so much time rationalizing that he never actually gets down to the task in hand. If the top phalange is markedly longer, the subject will act before thinking.

### Waisted phalange (Fig. 4. 10b)

The energies are knocked from one side to the other before reaching the willpower. These subjects are analytical, subtle thinkers who can look beneath the surface of life. They hate to swallow anything whole, but need to question and ponder over things. They lack practicality and tend to be intellectual or spiritual.

It is interesting to watch these two types in discussion. The thick phalange will say that he saw this or read that, while the waisted phalange says that, in his experience, he discovered . . .

## Print Patterns on the Thumb

*Whorl*
Selfish, original, ambitious.

*Loop*
Team worker, adaptable, pleasant, conventional.

*Arch*
Withdrawn, shy, restricted personality.

*Double loop*
Tries to please everyone at once, likes people but needs own company. May be psychic.

## The Base of the Thumb

This is the powerhouse of the thumb, where its energies are stored. It is part of the mount of Venus, so it represents feelings and desires before they are put into action. Venus embraces the physical world and the life force. Therefore, the thicker that mount the more forceful the personality, while the thinner mount is diplomatic and ready to give way to others. This shows whether the subject is logical or instinctive, tactful or thoughtless.

The area all around the base of the thumb, leading down towards the heel of the hand both on the back and the front, can be used to assess stamina, resistance to disease and the strength of the subject both in terms of health and of temperament. The mount of Venus is the storehouse of the body's reserves of energy. It is encircled by the life line which is itself associated with the physical and mental health of the subject. The "mouse" is the area which can be seen and felt at the *back* of the thumb when the hand is closed.

## The Mouse

### Healthy mouse (Fig. 4.11)

A large, firm mouse suggests a subject whose current state of health is fine. He has natural resistance to disease in addition to powers of recovery from illness. By nature he is restless, assertive, possibly even aggressive, and he is only really happy when working in a demanding job. If the head line is firm and straight with a well-developed Jupiter finger, there will be good executive abilities. If the knuckle of dexterity is well shaped and the percussion also well developed this subject would make a successful competitive sportsman.

If the mount of Venus is high and firm when

Figure 4.11

the hand is relaxed, there will be a good flow of blood through the circulatory system. The fingernails should have well developed moons for a strong constitution. These people are robust and passionate. They enjoy sports and other outdoor activities which give them the opportunity to sop up some of their ample energy and release some of their natural aggression in competition with others. They can be selfish, putting their own interests first, being in too much of a hurry to get on with life to stop in mid-stream and deal with the wants of others.

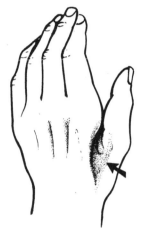

Figure 4.12

### Weak mouse (Fig. 4.12)

A floppy mouse points to a *currently* poor state of health, possibly someone who is recovering from illness or an operation or who has a generally weak constitution. A flat mount of Venus belongs to someone who likes to keep the mind occupied rather than take part in physical exercise. If the mount of Venus is exceptionally thin and soft, the subject is either lethargic or he has a particularly inward-looking nervous type of temperament. These people are sometimes cold and indifferent, unable to give or receive love, especially if the heart line is weak-looking, short, or does not curve upwards at all.

### Sickness (Fig. 4.13)

If when the hand is relaxed there is a definite hollow where a muscle should be this would imply muscle atrophy which could be the indicator of oncoming disease. Look at the major lines for signs of any neurological changes; if there are none, then look for diabetes.

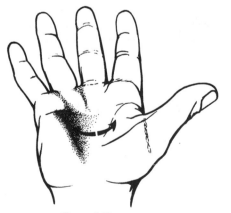

Figure 4.13

# CHAPTER FIVE

# THE LANGUAGE OF GESTURE

## How the fingers are held and used

It is always interesting to see how people use their hands and how their hands are placed when relaxed. A palmist can learn a great deal by creating a calm atmosphere during the reading and then glancing from time to time at the client's hands. It may even be possible to work out why someone has come to visit while you are still at the stage of putting the client at ease.

You may find it difficult to place your own fingers in some of the poses that we show. But if you acquire the habit of watching other people's hands, you will see that hands *do* fall naturally into these shapes. Take notice of people who are under stress or those who are relaxed. Watch your friends on social occasions when they are happy, when angry or irritable. There is no research like your own research, so talk to people whose hands seem to fall into odd poses, check to see what mood they are in and what is on their mind.

A palmist must compare both of the subject's hands closely. The dominant hand will show the *current* situation, worries and problems, while the minor hand will show the *underlying* influences, problems and the subject's habitual manner of thinking. When a client first comes in to the room, he may hold his hands in one way, then later, when confident, he could hold them quite differently.

## Fingers Held Straight or Curved into a Fist (Fig. 5.1)

A   Fingers that are held straight out show that the subject is self-assured, easy to get along with and optimistic. He may be a touch reckless. People whose fingers are displayed open are receptive to new ideas and they do not prejudge.

B   If the top phalanges are curled over a little the subject is self-assured, but common sense gives him a slightly more cautious attitude when in unfamiliar situations. If all the fingers are jammed tightly together with no light showing between them, the subject is holding back until he has assessed the situation. When he relaxes, he will loosen the fingers and let light through.

C   If the first and second phalanges are curved, the subject feels that he is not walking on safe ground, he is not sure of his facts. If the fingers are also held tightly together, he is self-absorbed and slightly introverted.

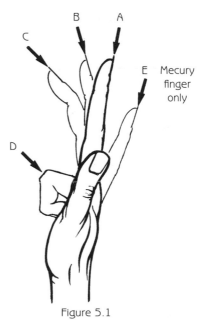

Figure 5.1

D   When the hands are tightly clenched, the subject is desperate, hopeless. If the fingers are also held tightly together, he is unable to cope with life and afraid of showing any emotion for fear of criticism, rejection or even violence. If in addition the thumb is tucked into the hand, the subject is probably close to a nervous breakdown. People who work with severely maltreated and unhappy children are familiar with the sight of a tucked-in thumb. It is a sign of self-protection in the face of extreme circumstances.

E   If the Mercury finger falls behind, away from the others, in the fashion of a Victorian lady holding a teacup, then the subject is self-contained and stubborn. There is very little desire to give and take and there is only one standpoint, which is his own. If there is a strong thumb, then the subject's mind has been long since made up and he is always sure of the rightness of his own opinions.

## Spacing Between Fingers

The spaces between the fingers are usually uneven; some fingers cling together, some wander off on their own. Take a look at both hands and compare the spacing while they are relaxed.

## Space Between Jupiter and Saturn Fingers (Fig. 5.2)

This is the active and outgoing radial side of the hand that shows the ability to think for oneself. This subject may listen to advice but in the last resort he always needs to make his own decisions.

If the Mercury and Apollo fingers curl over into a slight fist shape, the emotional side of life is difficult. This person may have a disappointing home life or may find personal relations difficult, although when at work he performs well and feels in control of the situation. This kind of hand may belong to the hardworking owner of a small business who loves the day-to-day challenge of work but either tunes out when at home or is rarely at ease in personal or emotional situations.

Figure 5.2

Figure 5.3

## Saturn and Apollo Fingers Held Closely Together (Fig. 5.3)

This type of posture is very commonly seen nowadays, and it shows the need for security and understanding. If the subject has a strong thumb, he will be able to stand up for himself and be able to cope. There could be conflict between the demands of family and career, or there could be a desire to work primarily for job satisfaction rather than just for money.

## Space Between Saturn and Apollo

This person may be a loner, the type who lives in the past and hates planning for the future. The characteristic V shape where the top two phalanges are apart shows signs of rebelliousness. This person probably did not fit in while at school. If there are whorl patterns on the fingertips then this person is not a team worker.

## Space Between Apollo and Mercury Fingers (Fig. 5.4)

This represents the ability to act independently. Watch these people while they are speaking, because they will be putting their own interpretation on the conversation. The conductor of an orchestra who holds his Mercury finger away from the others will interpret the music to reflect his own ideas. These people also need to get away from other people from time to time to recharge their mental batteries. There could be a sense of loneliness here.

Figure 5.4

## Fingertips Resting Lightly on a Table (Fig. 5.5)

This is the same basic shape as Fig. 5.3. Notice that the Jupiter and Saturn fingers are more arched. The arched Jupiter signifies an inner lack of confidence and Saturn some inadequacy when coping with everyday problems. There is also a need for security and understanding. It is by looking at these details that the palmist begins to build up a mental picture of his subject's abilities, weaknesses and the depth of his feelings.

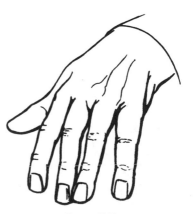

Figure 5.5

## A Woman's Hand 1 (Fig. 5.6)

The fingers here are evenly spaced but curved, so they show an open mind. The Jupiter finger is more curved than the others suggesting uncertainty. The subject wants the palmist to tell her the truth about herself and her life and she will not hide anything from him. The thumb that is lying close to the hand shows a desire to cooperate rather than to push herself forward.

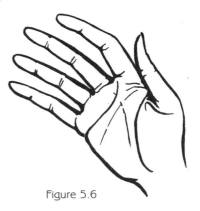

Figure 5.6

## A Woman's Hand 2 (Fig. 5.7)

Similar to Fig. 5.6, but this time the fingers are held close together and straight. The thumb is sticking out. People like this can be seen on television discussion programs. They are confident, and their closed fingers show that they do not want to be questioned or contradicted. Their minds close down so as to fend off criticism or to hide any sign of inadequacy. They do not wish to show emotion because they think it a sign of weakness. If the thumb is held away from the hand, they wish to be seen as being in charge. If the first phalange of the thumb turns back they may *appear* to be assertive and extroverted but this may be covering shyness, selfish motives or greed.

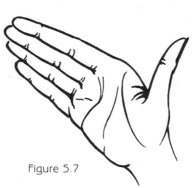

Figure 5.7

## A Woman's Hand (Fig. 5.8)

This illustration shows limp hands turned inwards toward each other. This posture is a nervous defensive reaction that shows that the emotional energy level is low. It would be a good idea to look at the life line in the minor hand for corroboration of this. Note the left hand is massaging the thumb of the right—this is a form of

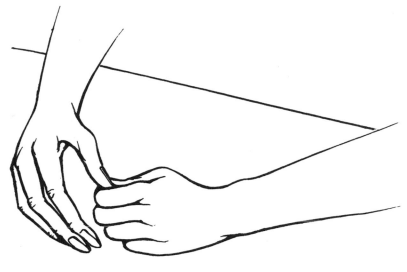

Figure 5.8

reflexology. You can often see people massaging their fingertips while thinking what to say.

## Hands on the Table (Fig. 5.9)

A man sits before you and places his hands on the table. The spaces between the fingers in both hands are equal, indicating a balanced open mind. It is rare that one actually finds fingers equally spaced

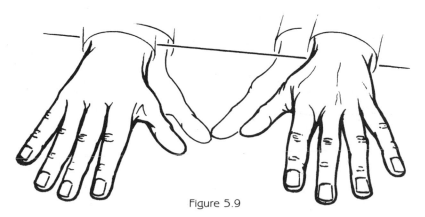

Figure 5.9

like these. If he chooses to lay his hands flat on the table this shows that the inner and outer self are balanced and the mind is relaxed. If the palms are raised a little this means he is conscious of his surroundings and environment.

Arched hands show uncertainty. If the hands are placed wide apart, this is a sign of an active nature—a person who likes to get things moving. The closer the hands are placed, the more thought he will give before acting. If the two thumbs are extended and touching each other and both hands are aligned symmetrically, this person is unconsciously aware of everything that is happening in his environment, every movement in the room. He could overreact to a situation and sometimes pick up on irrelevant details.

## Hand Language

- People who are trying to convince others or to sell something, use their hands in a "giving" motion whilst at the same time nodding their heads.
- When someone appears to be "washing" their hands, they are under severe distress.
- A sign of desperation occurs when the thumbs are tucked tightly in and the arms held stiffly down at the sides. This behavior is most noticeable among children who are terrified and miserable. If adults display this behavior, they are either under the ultimate kind of stress or being abused.
- An open palm is used to prove friendly intentions and it is an automatic gesture which shows that they are not carrying a weapon.
- Those who want to be understood "plead" with their hands, but this device is also used by the manipulative person.
- A "roly-poly" or "stacking-up" motion with the hands held in front tells that the subject is desperate to be understood. If he is being deliberately misunderstood, the motions become wilder.
- People who wag their Jupiter finger are being bossy.
- Sometimes curled hands are due to the person having very dry skin.

# CHAPTER SIX

# ENERGY RHYTHMS: TIMING

## An Introduction to the Lines

There is a common belief that the body renews itself every seven years. There is no real foundation for this belief. Indeed, we know that some parts of the body, such as bone, change very slowly after puberty, whilst the soft tissue restores itself rapidly—especially the liver. Nevertheless, there does seem to be some basis for this, even if it is only a kind of imaginary psychological timing mechanism.

This arbitrary rhythm shows up in a sudden increase in the number of lines that arrive on the hand adjacent to the fate line or the Apollo line at particular points along their paths. The body seems to build up an excess of nervous, emotional and physical energies that need to be released somewhere. These energies can galvanize people into action and cause them to change their lives in a positive way. A marriage that has never been good can suddenly feel stifling at these tension-filled times, causing the subject to make that long dreamed of break or to take up with someone else. It is also amazing how these times can actually coincide with external events such as redundancy, promotion, the birth of a child or the spouse walking out. If the energy is suppressed for too long, pressure builds up that will cause unusual behavior or be internalized into mental or physical ailments. This energy will find any seat of weakness in the body and exploit it, just as the wind and tides will work away at cracks in a sea wall, ultimately bringing down the whole structure.

One must look at the life line and head line to find out which way this will affect the subject. If there are many lines at the top of the hand, there will be a surge in old age which will be too much for the body to take, so this would probably cause the subject to die quite suddenly. Fig. 6.1 gives a suggestion of the kind of wave pattern that can be seen on a hand.

We suggest that you take a look at a few hand prints and then draw horizontal bands across them to show the sections that are "busy." The more of these energy lines, the more tension the subject has to cope with. An indication of a positive use of this energy is in the effort lines that rise upwards from the life line. These lines can give some valuable clues to the timing of the rhythm in each individual hand.

## Energy Rhythms Beside the Fate and Apollo Lines (Fig. 6.1)

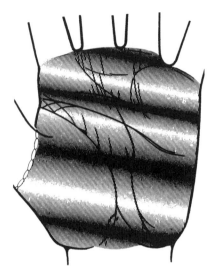

Figure 6.1   Energy rhythms

A  One long, thick companion line gives purpose to the person's ambitions.

B  Two or more short, strong companion lines symbolize change, ambition, restlessness and desires.

C  Many fine lines around Apollo show that the subject is searching for the way forward. He is apprehensive and using more energy than the body is producing (look for dots to substantiate this). The searching and apprehension could involve a questioning of the subject's whole way of life—but it is the *emotional*, relating, family side of life that is probably the uppermost problem.

D  Many fine lines around the fate line may indicate freelance work or stretched physical and financial resources. The subject could be taking on too many obligations. These could be chores or financial obligations.

E  Many fine lines at the top of the palm are a sign of activity creating energy. These people like to keep busy later in life, thereby remaining fit and spry well into old age. If the lines go up into the fingers, the person becomes cantankerous in old age.

## Timing on the Hand

Many palmistry books try to show the passage of time on the hands by dividing the lines up into equal segments, but the hand isn't a mechanical instrument, so timing cannot be calibrated in this manner. Joys and sorrows that are particularly intense appear to take a longer period of time to occur on the hand than they do in real life. The impact of an experience upon the mind and body leaves its mark, just as the memory of the trauma lingers. It remains in the hand when subsequent, less emotive events have long been forgotten. As we grow older the years appear to fly by, and this is reflected in the crowded spacing of the years at the northern end of the palm.

## The Life Line and Fate Line

This is complex because both lines influence each other at the southern end of the hand. The timing goes *down* the life line for health and energy, and *up* the hand when influenced by the events that are shown on the fate line.

## The Life Line and the Head Line

The section of the head line that is under the Jupiter and Saturn fingers shows the competition between the requirements of the mind and the body while the subject is in the process of growing up.

## Quick Method of Timing on the Hand

Look at the hand with the fingers together and the thumb relaxed and away from the hand.

*(Fig. 6.2)*
A line dropped down from the middle of the Jupiter finger meets the life line at approximately 15–17 years of age.

*(Fig. 6.3)*
A line dropped down between the Jupiter and Saturn fingers meets the life line at approximately 22–25 years of age.

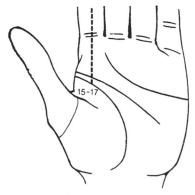

Figure 6.2

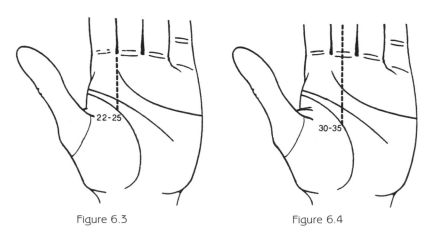

Figure 6.3                    Figure 6.4

*(Fig. 6.4)*
A line dropped down the middle of the Saturn finger meets the life line at approximately 30–35 years.

*(Fig. 6.5)*
Draw an imaginary line across the hand from the angle of dexterity and at right angles to the line dropping down from Saturn. This represents approximately 45 years of age on the life line but only 23–25 years on the fate line.

*(Fig. 6.6)*
Take two more equal spaces down the life line to reach the age of 55–60 years; this corresponds to 20–23 years on the fate and life

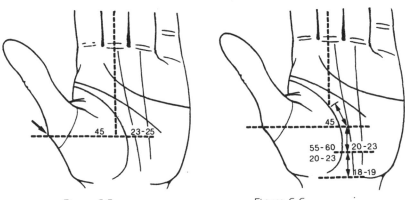

Figure 6.5                    Figure 6.6

lines. The next equal spacing down the life line will take you to the age of 18–19 years on the fate line only.

## Life Line and Fate Line (Fig. 6.7)

There is a definite relationship between the life line and the fate line at around the age of 20. Therefore an island at that point can suggest a low depressive period at the age of 20 and an illness at around 60.

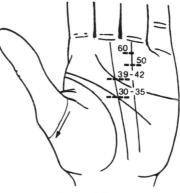

The age of 30–35 years is reached on the fate line at the point where it meets the head line. The age of 39–42 years is reached on the fate line where it meets the heart line. Half way between the heart line and the crease line at the bottom of the Apollo finger is 50 years of age; three-quarters of the way between the heart line and the crease at the bottom of the Apollo finger is 60 years of age.

Figure 6.7

## Timing on the Family Line (Fig. 6.8)

This follows the arc of the *life line* downwards.

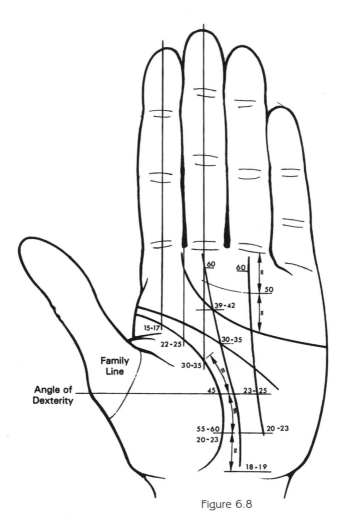

Figure 6.8

# CHAPTER SEVEN

# THE MAJOR LINES AND ZONES

## An Introduction to the Lines on the Hand

For centuries palmists have enjoyed talking about lines on the hand, giving them names and characteristics, sometimes with barely a glance at the picture they really portray. Lines are controlled by the nerve endings. They give a physical computer printout of the life and development of each one of us. The lines show our order of priorities and the value that we award ourselves and also our activities. They pick out the environmental influences upon us, add our reaction to those around us, and indicate the depth of the feelings we have toward our mate, family and friends. They display our dedication to a career or job and our ability to handle it.

## How to Look at the Lines on the Hand

Try to imagine the lines as a river of energy flowing from the wrist to the fingers. Deep lines can cope with more power; this makes for a positive type of personality. Lines that are unblemished and fairly straight offer no resistance to the flow of energies. This gives purpose to the personality and makes for a relatively trouble-free life.

## Continuous Lines

These show continuity in life. An unbroken fate line belongs to someone who stays for years in the same job. An unbroken Apollo line belongs to someone who remains in the same house or area for years. An unbroken life line tells much the same story. These people do not break new ground.

## Bends in the Lines

These show the movement of life's vital forces to be slower and more changeable.

## Lines that Merge or Run Parallel

These are helpful signs on the hand.

## A Line that Splits into a "Y" Shape

A dividing of the ways. This shows where there are decisions to be taken and choices to be made.

## Islands

Energy that is split in two different directions, also difficulties in life depending on where the island is found.

## Very Fine Major Lines

The energy flow is restricted, so this person is likely to be very touchy.

## A Hand With Clear Cut Lines

This subject has old-fashioned values and likes to conform. There usually is a strong straight health line.

## Tassels, Squares, Crosses etc.

Please see the individual chapter sections on each of the relevant lines.

## Transverse Lines

Awkward influences put upon people by others, problems, setbacks and decisions.

## Dots on Any Line

These are always important, and their effect can be judged by the places where they are found. Dots are small craters that suck away energy from the line they are situated on. This shows anguish, anxiety or physical stress, illness, etc.

## Many Fine Lines Grouped Around a Line or Replacing it Altogether at Some Point

These could be termed "searching lines" because they demonstrate the age at which the confusion occurs and the sphere of life that is affected. At this particular point in time, people cannot see the wood for the trees, so they waste valuable strength thinking of all the possibilities. They may react by overeating, drinking or taking drugs without doing anything positive to sort out their problems. This kind of situation is commonly found on the fate line. If the subject actually tackles these problems in a positive manner, it is amazing how quickly these tiny lines appear to peel themselves off the hands leaving just two or three stronger and more determined lines.

## Colored Patches of Skin on the Lines

When a hand has a minimum of lines and an area of skin with a brownish patch, the subject's life is not fully under his control during the period of time shown on the hand. The subject may have had a spell in the services or even in prison. There may be a period of depression or a serious health problem. There are other marks that indicate these specific problems, namely, peculiarly shaped islands which show the experienced palmist periods of time when the subject felt enclosed and shut off from normal life. This *could* be caused by a spell in prison or in hospital. Another example would be a woman who felt shut in and unhappy while at home with small children. Obviously this situation could feel like a prison to one woman but be a time of joy for another.

## Do the Lines on the Hand Change?

When a palmist looks at a hand, he sees the picture of the subject's life *at the time of the reading*. Lines grow, weaken and disappear altogether. Health problems cause some lines to dive under the skin or fade away, especially the fate or Apollo lines. Small vertical lines under the skin may change color.

## Basic Information

A long, healthy-looking life line allows the energies to flow easily along its length, giving the lucky subject the prospect of a healthy, happy life with little or nothing to worry about. The line should have a deeper color than the rest of the palm when the hand is stretched. Look at both hands to see if there are any differences between them. A trauma that is obvious on the minor hand and all but invisible on the dominant one shows that there has been a difficult experience in the past. The subject has forgotten about this, but because it is still marked on the minor hand, we can see that it remains in the subconscious mind.

## Inner and Outer Life (Fig. 7.1)

Remember, hands change all the time in subtle ways and sometimes quite dramatically. The minor hand shows what our inner selves want while the dominant hand shows the adaptations that we make. If for instance, the life line on the minor hand reaches out into the palm, while on the dominant hand it tucks around the mount of Venus, there will be a *desire* to travel. This person will want to be adventurous and to seek a different way of life from that of the subject's parents. The dominant hand shows a conventional stay-at-home life but more success in relationships.

Figure 7.1  Lines can come and go

## Having it All (Fig. 7.2)

If the life line divides widely at the lower end with one branch curving around Venus and the other reaching out into the palm, the subject could desire both a secure home life and a job which allows him to travel and have interesting experiences. If this is shown on both hands, he will have it all.

## Beginnings

Figure 7.2

A life line that begins high up near Jupiter *(Fig. 7.3a)* or throws small branches upward at its start indicates both idealism and ambition. If the line also hugs the mount of Venus fairly closely, the person will be intellectual, idealistic and ambitious rather than instinctive. If the line starts lower down and curves flatly around Venus *(Fig. 7.3b)* the person will be full of life, both home loving and sociable, also ambitious, probably sexy and intuitive in an instinctive, self-preserving sort of way. For a life line that is tied to the head line, please refer to the section on the head line.

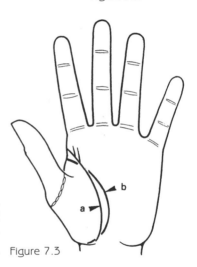

Figure 7.3

Islands near the start of the life line show troubles in childhood and youth. There is a myth that heavy islands at the very beginning of the life line on the radial edge show some mystery surrounding the subject's birth *(Fig. 7.4)*. Facts seem to bear this out, as we have come across a woman whose mother had deliberately registered her at birth as being illegitimate in order to hurt and humiliate her perfectly legitimate father!

Straightforward islands are likely to be caused by illness, and a large rather isolated island would indicate a fairly lengthy spell in hospital. A gap between the life and head lines with crisscross lines,

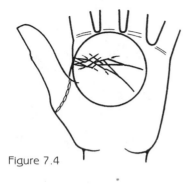

Figure 7.4

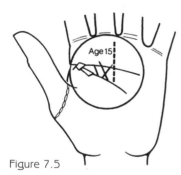

Figure 7.5

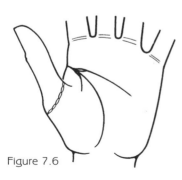

Figure 7.6

islands or short harsh lines barring the way *(Fig. 7.5)* suggests that the subject was probably looked after by someone other than his parents as a child and was not happy with the arrangement. Unhappiness at school is shown by a "cat's cradle" effect in this area.

An island or a sudden parting of the ways between the head and life lines with a strong line dropping down from inside the life line *(Fig. 7.6)* shows a traumatic change of situation during childhood. The dropping line indicates a loss that is consistent with death in the family, parents splitting up, a move of house or a change of school. The subject lost something that was familiar and had to adjust quickly to a new situation.

## Middle

This is the section where effort lines frequently appear; their position shows the age at which the subject makes any special effort in life. Events on the life line are often mirrored on the head line *(Fig. 7.7)*, the heart line and elsewhere. It is a case of collecting evidence to see what the effort relates to. If there is a corresponding upward hook on the head line or a new beginning on the fate line, there could be promotion or a better job. If the effort line comes at the end of an island or weak patch in the line, it will show that there is a period of illness or emotional suffering from which the person emerges somewhat older and wiser *(Fig. 7.8)*. The person will make an effort to overcome his problems. It does not matter where these effort lines lead, but the struggle is probably harder (and more worthwhile) if the lines go toward Saturn.

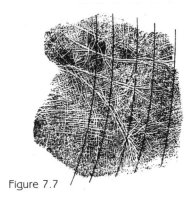

Figure 7.7

## Short Life Line (Fig. 7.9)

Many people have broken life lines or life lines that appear to be exceptionally short. In practically every case, the fate line becomes a second life line *(Fig. 7.9)*. This picture shows some kind of upsetting change in the subject's life. The most common event these days is divorce. The life line has a good deal to do with location and where we put down roots, so a divorce that involves a change of home circumstances is bound to effect this line.

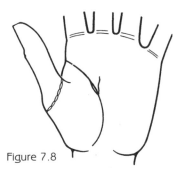

Figure 7.8

## Case History: Paul and Brenda (Fig. 7.10)

Paul and Brenda were married. They both had the same formation of a foreshortened life line that seemed to end at the same age point. Their fate lines then took over from the life line. It was obvious that both their lives would change drastically due to an event that would affect both of them at

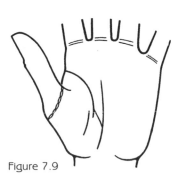

Figure 7.9

Figure 7.10

the same time. The marriage wasn't a happy one, and some time later Paul discovered that Brenda was having an affair, so Paul decided to leave Brenda and their children.

It is worth noting that outward jumps on the life line usually show that the subject is being pushed into focusing on work. Paul had to push ahead with his career in order to afford two homes, especially when he subsequently remarried and started a new family. Brenda has not married again but has developed a successful career for herself, which certainly was not how she had expected her life to proceed. This just goes to show that a short life line is definitely not an indicator of an early death, but the death of a situation. (Tarot readers will equate this to the Death card, which has much the same interpretation.)

In addition to moving over to other parts of the hand, a short life line is often supported by extra lines appearing on the mount of Venus. These extra lines strengthen the life line and help the person both to get over the problem and give added physical reserves of strength. Friends and family are shown to help at that time. The backing line could be a line of Mars, a medial line or just a stray reinforcement line.

## The Lower Zone of the Life Line and the Line of Mars (Fig. 7.11)

The appearance of this extra line indicates a renewed interest in home and domesticity later in life. A man who has spent his life out at work may retire and find unexpected pleasures in the home and surrounding area. A woman who has struggled with a career and family may be able at last to relax and find pleasure in gardening,

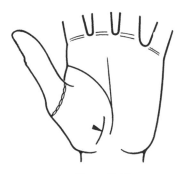

Figure 7.11

cooking or sewing. The priorities turn to the home, security and emotional understanding.

## Return to Home Life (Fig. 7.12)

If circumstances have made the subject into a career person as a result of a divorce, then remarriage could provide a pleasant and comfortable home situation later in life. It is worth looking at the loyalty line (a) to see if this points towards the southern end of the life line, and also at changes on the Apollo line and secondary attachment lines. If the new line of Mars that backs up the life line at this point has a Y formation on it (b), this is also a sign of remarriage.

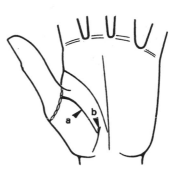

Figure 7.12

## Giving up on Life

If the life line becomes wispy, tasseled or breaks up into fragments, the subject will either give up on life, preferring to sit back and do nothing, or he may have weak health later in life. This *might* indicate early death, but one must check the lines at the top of the hand to see if life continues. If the life line fades away and then renews itself, there will be a period of weakness followed by a return to health and strength.

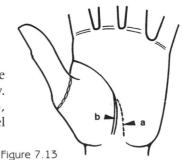

## Splits (Fig. 7.13)

Splits on the southern end of the life line mean some sort of divided loyalty. This can range from the wide split (a), showing a strong home life plus travel

Figure 7.13

and a career, to the narrow split (b) of a mother struggling to work and cope with a young family.

A line that curves around Venus would imply that the subject remains close to the place where he was born and also close to his parents. If there is a split, there will still be contact with the parental family and although the ideas and philosophy of the two generations could be very different, there would be humorous tolerance between them. When the line sweeps out into the hand, the subject will most probably move far away from his place of birth and/or could have widely divergent attitudes to those of his family. They may never be able to see eye to eye—if they see each other at all!

Reading *up* the life line, there could be an early illness that has later repercussions, such as rheumatic fever. There may, on the other hand, be a niggling complaint later in life. Splits indicate a split in energies, so these may refer to health, location or a desire to be in two places at once. Check if there are two family rings, two strong Apollo lines or any other signs of double interests.

## The Head Line

The head line shows how we use our mind. It can point out damage to the head, throat, neck, shoulders and upper respiratory region or to mental disturbances. It shows the habitual manner of thinking and gives information about schooling, studies and the shape of the career.

## A Gap Between the Head and Life Lines (Fig. 7.14)

This is supposed to indicate an early break from the parents and an independent attitude and that may be the case. However, this can signify an easy-going relationship between the generations and parents who gave approval and who encouraged the subject to think for himself and to be himself. The subject can take chances in life because he is not

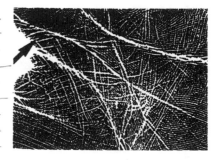

Figure 7.14

tied to tradition or to the ways of his parents. He may leave home early or just be allowed to be himself and develop his personality in a free and easy way. The other meaning is that the person had little to do with his parents during childhood and was forced to become an independent thinker earlier than he wanted.

## Beginning (Fig. 7.15)

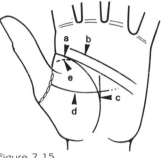

A tied head line (a) occurs where the head and life line are joined for about a half an inch (12 mm) or more at their starting point. This belongs to a cautious person who is slow to cut the apron strings or one who spends much of his life being pressurized by one or both of his parents. A gap between the head and life lines (b) shows a more adventurous person who either leaves home early or has a free and easy relationship with the Figure 7.15
parents. For confirmation of family pressure check to see if the life and fate lines are also joined at the southern end (c) and if there are irritation lines radiating outwards from the mount of Venus (d). An exceptionally timid person might have a head line which starts *inside* the life line on the mount of Mars (e).

## Early Struggles (Figs. 7.16 and 7.17)

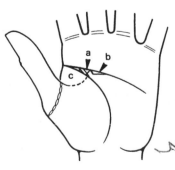

Islands, bars and jagged, triangular markings at this point show illness or unhappiness in childhood. Small lines that try to bind together (a) show unhappiness while at school or college *(Fig. 7.17)*. The subject may have hated school, or alternatively loved school and seen it as an outlet and escape from the home. It is possible to spot how old the person was during this time of unhappiness by the posi-

Figure 7.16

tion of this effect. If a middle-aged man has a large, triangular or diamond-shaped island just where the head and life line part (b), try asking him if he did any kind of military service. He may have enjoyed this, especially if the nearby mount of lower Mars is full (c).

Figure 7.17

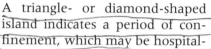
A triangle- or diamond-shaped island indicates a period of confinement, which may be hospitalization, a bad job, difficult home life or even a period in some sort of institution. This island shows that the subject felt imprisoned, even if he could have made a move but simply accepted the situation.

## Islands and Effort Lines (Fig. 7.18)

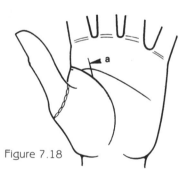

Figure 7.18

A classic giveaway for unhappiness or lack of satisfaction at secondary school is the appearance of effort lines on the life line (a) as soon as the life line becomes free of the head line.

If the head line rises or throws up effort lines here, the person is delighted to leave his adolescence and his school days behind him. He begins to blossom intellectually and to take the first meaningful strides in his career.

## Middle Part of the Head Line (Fig. 7.19)

This is the practical section of the head line. A strong clear line shows a good mind and healthy upper-body area. A wavy line (a) shows that the subject has difficulty in sustaining mental

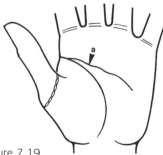

Figure 7.19

effort. He will go through periods where he makes great efforts in life and low periods where he becomes depressed. He probably reacts to life rather than trying to create a comfortable personal lifestyle.

## Straight Head Line (Fig. 7.20)

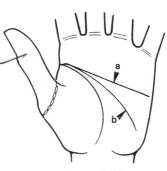

It used to be said that mathematicians have straight head lines (a) while linguists have sloping ones and artistic people ultra sloping ones (b). That view is too restricted, but it does make sense, because when the line runs straight across the hand, the person thinks in black and white. Look at the second phalange of the thumb to see whether it is long, which indicates logical thinking, or short, which suggests idiosyncratic thinking. This subject

Figure 7.20

prefers a practical career that offers security and normality. He may find it hard to understand or express feelings and he may lack imagination. If the line runs towards the percussion, he could be aggressive. A long straight line keeps this subject working to the end of his days because work offers him companionship, respect and self-respect in addition to a steady income. This is a team member rather than a boss.

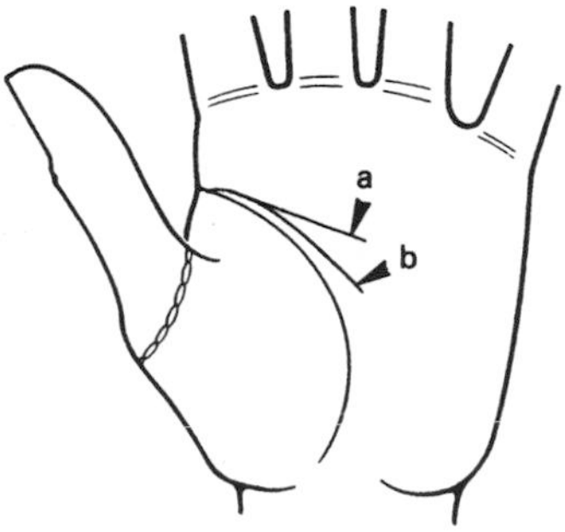

Figure 7.21

## The Long and the Short of the Head Line (Fig. 7.21)

When the line is short and straight (a), there is deep concentration in a narrow field. This person could go far because determined ambition, coupled with his ability to focus on specific goals, pushes him to the top. Malcolm has found this kind of line on the hand of a super civil servant who was very adept at filling out complicated forms. When Malcolm was faced with these forms, he struggled with them, and the lady couldn't see why he should have had this problem.

This type likes to be in charge of others but he also needs the esteem of other people. (Check fingertips for whorls that indicate a loner, loops for sociability and small, blue-colored spatulate nails for tension and ambition.) This intense concentration may have nothing to do with the subject's job, but it might be poured into a hobby or interest. The only way to explain anything to this type is in terms of his own specialization. He will not understand anyone else's points of reference and will scoff at everything that is outside his own field of knowledge. We have tried to work out whether this type has a sense of humor but when we asked such subjects, they didn't think it was funny!

## The Sloping Head Line (Fig. 7.22)

A slight slope brings a nice balance between practicality and imagination (a). This person has a mixture of inter-ests and does not just live for work. He enjoys company and conversation. A steeper slope belongs to someone who is able to understand people intuitive-ly, so he may work as a salesman, per-sonnel officer or counselor. He may have artistic or musical talent; he may love travel or the countryside. If the slope is very steep the imagination and intuition are highly developed (c). A mother who has this kind of line would weave fabulous bedtime tales for her children, but she could also be temperamental and touchy. A sloping head line is a double-edged sword, because it endows talent and creativity but also moodiness, over-sensitivity and childhood fears and phobias. This slightly unworldly person needs to be alone from time to time, so that he can meditate and retreat from the world. He has a tendency to sop up other people's sorrows, espe-cially if there is also a girdle of Venus on the hand. A short sloping line (b) belongs to the lazy thinker, someone who does not make much effort, does not want to learn and jumps from one idea to another.

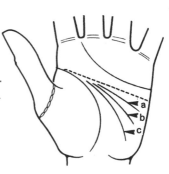

Figure 7.22

## The End of the Head Line (Fig. 7.23)

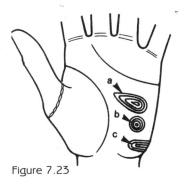

If, in addition to a long head line, there is a skin-ridge loop on Luna (a), the subject could have considerable success in some sort of creative work (see head line print figures 7.29 and 7.30). He has a good memory that may help him in his work. A whorl on Luna (b) would add mediumistic tendencies and a loop low on Pluto (c), or entering Luna from the percussion, would put him in tune with nature or the sea.

Figure 7.23

## Creative Head and Life Lines (Fig. 7.24)

If the head line runs parallel to a life line that reaches out for Luna, there will be success as a writer or an artist.

## Branches and Hooks (Fig. 7.25)

- A head line that turns upwards (a) is not often seen but it shows success in business and often also a great sense of humor.
- When the head and heart lines are close to each other (b) the emotions cloud the thinking and the person might be intolerant, but when they are widely spaced the person is calculating and he could be a dangerous adversary.

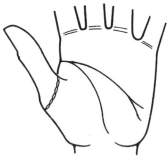

Figure 7.24

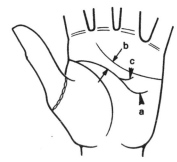

Figure 7.25

- Upward branches (c) are a form of mental self-help showing efforts to improve life. Branches that are exceptionally strong and travel directly towards Mercury signify an effort to learn and communicate. They may also relate to business matters.
- Other upward branches have no specific meaning except to show times of effort.
- Downward branches imply times of struggle and loss, but some are fork formations rather than branches. If a fork is as strong as the head line itself, there is an imaginative approach. Traditionally this is called the writer's fork.

## Simian Line (Fig. 7.40)

This is a strong straight line that cuts across the hand, combining and compressing the normal head and heart line. Tradition has it that monkeys have this line, hence its name. Tradition also has it that people with Down's syndrome have these lines but neither of these ideas is true. About one person in fifteen has this kind of mark and it shows intense concentration, possibly obsession, regarding some part of their lives. They might get their feeling side and their thinking sides a bit mixed up. The feelings and emotions are held under heavy control and the line separates the two halves of the hands. This causes the intuitive side (Neptune/Luna) to be parted from the affections and desires (heart line and mounts). Semi-simian lines place pressure on the emotions and they may be associated with people who find it difficult to give or to find love. These people find it hard to concentrate on both work and relationships at the same time.

## Forks, Marks and Endings (Fig. 7.26)

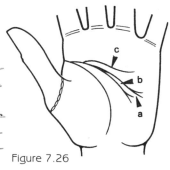

- Tasselled endings (a) may show a lack of calcium, fluoride, potassium or just a great deal of worry. They may also indicate senile dementia, but look at the life line to see if it is also weak toward the southern end.

Figure 7.26

- A clear and strong line ending in one or two splits (b) shows that the person will continue to work into old age but the work may be part-time, voluntary or there may be many interests late in life. (Check the upper ends of the fate and Apollo lines.)
- Heavily forked, split or doubled head lines (c) have a number of meanings, all of which take some living with. The traditional meaning is of a split personality but these people are probably simply multi-talented with a combination of practicality and imagination.
- Two parallel lines allow the subject to explore two completely different facets of his personality. A good example would be of an accountant who was also a champion ballroom dancer, and it is possible that his co-workers would not even know of his hobby. He also has a good head for business. This subject may chase too many rainbows and (especially if both hands have this formation) find it hard to finish a task without being diverted by something more interesting. Catch him on a good day and he can be great fun, but on a bad day he will be angry and disappointed with himself.
- Islands, bars, breaks, etc., denote health problems or setbacks in the course of life. A fairly common sign is that of an island with an effort line rising out of it. This shows a period of worry, but the effort line shows us that the subject hauls himself out of the pit to make life worth living again.
- Breaks in the line may indicate problems related to work but also illness and accidents. A square that covers a break will show the problem has been averted. Light squares indicate periods of frustration, of being bored and fed up with life or with one's job. The effort line shows that the subject will eventually choose a more satisfying lifestyle.

## Chained Head Line (Fig. 7.27)

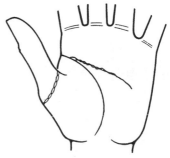

A chained line shows some kind of feeble-mindedness. This may range from an apathetic attitude to life and mental laziness to genuine mental handicap. Many small bars, or a patch of chaining, may indicate migraines,

Figure 7.27

or a temporarily tense situation. Dots and bars also indicate migraine, possibly eye strain or other head and neck problems.

The head line which rules every part of our lives signifies our capacity for learning and the way we think, but also how the nerves, emotions and energy rhythms affect our mental outlook at different stages of our lives. The life line is very much linked with the head line and feeds it the energy that it needs to keep it going. This is especially so when the head line is long.

## Repeated Patterns

Many people's hands have characteristics such as islands and chained effects that appear in an identical pattern on both the head and life lines. A chained and island effect at the beginning of the lines denotes a battle for energy between the brain and the body during youth.

## Examples

The following are all examples of real people and what their head lines (and other features) tell us.

## John (Fig. 7.28)

This is the story of John, a young man who will pour his energies into work rather than make a success of his marriage. He will deny the emotional demands of his wife and family, while pushing himself ahead in his career where he feels safe.

- John's head line slopes slightly but curls upward in the latter stages suggesting a long journey toward ultimate career success. The long head line keeps him striving, becoming more business-like and goal-orientated as life goes on. The combination of that long, strong head line with a comparatively weak-looking life line shows a lack of balance in his life. There will be periods of depression and occasional feelings of failure because his desires (head) are not matched by his physical ability to achieve them (life).
- The tatty-looking ending to the head line with a small line reaching out from the percussion to grasp it (a) shows insomnia.

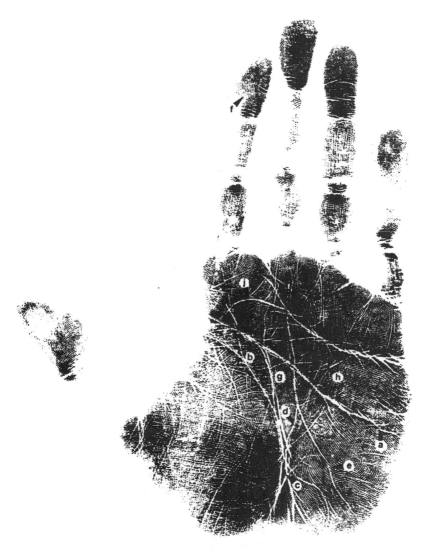

Figure 7.28

The life line is intertwined with other lines that impede its progress. The difference between a smooth clear life line and one that has other lines wrapping themselves up with it is comparable to the difference in driving seventy miles along a highway and seventy miles along a dirt road.

- The heavy line of restriction (b) suggests that John's parents are extraordinarily repressive and they may be the kind who believe in some kind of emotionally restrictive religion or they may insist on an arranged marriage. Both of these were so in John's case.

- An island tucked well into the middle of the life line (c) is evidence of emotional depression and unhappiness, at about twenty-two years of age. When a fate line remains tied to the life line along so much of its path (d), the parents continue to exert an influence when it is no longer appropriate.

- There is a break in the fate line and also an alteration of its course when his depression begins to interfere seriously with his work. Notice the inclining short Jupiter finger (f). At that time he was totally unsure of his direction in life due to the fact that until then his parents had taken his decisions for him. At the time of the reading his hands were too soft for a healthy young man suggesting a lack of energy.

- His mental and emotional problems are not over yet. At the point where he is aged thirty-five an island appears on both the head and fate lines (g), and there is a relationship or marriage split V in the Apollo line (h). Any V that appears in the center of the hand on the Apollo line will show marriage difficulties. This is followed by an energy rhythm at 38–40 years, lots of searching lines. The head line is relatively clear at this point, so he will put his energies into work. The line from the heart line (j) is a safety valve. He will be able to channel his excessive nervous and emotional energies into work.

- It appears as things stand now, that he will continue to do his duty to his wife and family and he will also make tremendous achievements in his career as a form of compensation. We can only speculate as to how much of this achievement is an unconscious and continuing desire to please and impress over-critical and over-demanding parents. How far would he be prepared to push himself if he were happily married? Once he becomes rich and successful, will he become vulnerable to someone who appears to offer the opportunity to fill in the gaps in his sexual and emotional experience? Can we change the scenario to allow him to fall in love with a woman of his choice and make a fresh start for himself? We cannot see any of these alternatives yet, but John is young, his character is still unformed and his lines will change. His life story does not have to be so depressing, but it may provide us with a truly memorable captain of industry.

## Ronald (Fig. 7.29)

Ronald has a curved, imaginative head line that curls upward toward the mount of Mercury. This shows that he is a clever businessman who can visualize how to achieve results. The life line shows abundant energy, while the clear fate line shows mental alertness and a sense of purpose. The loop formation on Luna near the end of the head line shows a pool of imaginative

Figure 7.29

energies from which he can draw. Because the head line reaches down to this pool, he can use it to bring artistic, creative and unusual methods of thinking to his work, but the drawback is that he thinks too long about problems. He may also find it difficult to separate his business interests from the emotional side of his life, or he may consider business problems from too emotional a standpoint.

At the age of twenty-seven the fate line forks, and a decision line from Venus creates a blockage, thereby forcing him to make decisions, some of which are emotional rather than practical. The fate line starts up again after this, but it jumps toward the ulna side, showing that his new beginning is something of a backward step and that his thinking is not as good as it was previously.

## Joanna (Fig. 7.30)

Figure 7.30

Joanna has a straight practical head line that means she likes her decisions to be clear-cut, hence also the strong and determined fate line. A strong life line that shows she will make a success of her career fuels these features. She has two loop formations on Luna representing two pools of creative energy which suggests that she needs a creative element in her career. Joanna is a qualified hairdresser who can visualize a finished hairstyle and then create it. The mount of Neptune is quite high, which links the imaginative Luna to the practical acquisitive, value-conscious Venus. She will go far.

## Paul (Fig. 7.31)

Paul has a crazily split head line. In his case, this does not imply brain damage because all the lines are joined at one point or another along their length. It means that Paul will start a job, become distracted, then start another and forget to finish the first. As he is in a position of some authority, one can imagine the confusion that he creates. Paul's head line is tied to the life line (a), showing

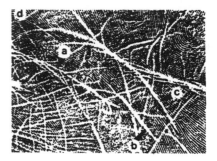

Figure 7.31

early sensitivity and reluctance to relinquish the state of childhood and his ties to his parents. The middle section (b) is where you would expect to find the practical side of the head line. This section has a V formation, which shows him to be unable to take decisions and preferring others to take them for him.

The third section (c) goes into the heart line and then curves over back to the head line. He is unsure of where his emotions lie. When part of the heart line goes into the head line (d) there is an uncertainty as to just what sex the subject feels himself to be. In Paul's case, he is married to the matronly type who keeps him in line. It seems that after reaching a reluctant adulthood, Paul has replaced his mother with a dominant mother-type figure.

## Michael (Fig. 7.32)

Michael's head line is tied to his life line (a) showing excessive timidity and a pessimistic attitude. He gives up too easily. The head line wavers and bends up and down, showing that he is indecisive, changeable. The fate line is used as part of the life line that signifies restriction, but it also suggests that the energies that he can muster will be channeled into work. The short head line, accompanied by a strong life line of roughly the same length and appearance, indicates that he is mentally normal, albeit at the lower end of the scale. The shortness of the lines shows that he can only concentrate his efforts on one small objective at a time. Michael will be virtually unable to make any normal social or emotional life for himself. He is just this side of being mentally handicapped.

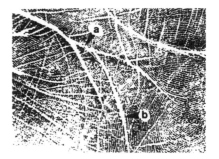

Figure 7.32

## The Heart Line

### Malcolm's tale

My first introduction to the value of palmistry was way back in my late teens. I went to a marriage guidance meeting with a girlfriend. The doctor giving the talk turned to the subject of "what makes a good lover." In my purity and innocence, I had not given it a thought. He said, "The man with short fingers is too fussy and full of routine to become a good lover, but on the other hand," he said, pointing at me, "a man with long fingers is romantic and would make a good lover." Needless to say, I promptly sat on my hands. Therefore, when looking at the heart line, look also at the *shape* of the hand.

## Basic Information

In the case of the head and life line it is best to have a clean clear line but a super-clear heart line would belong to someone who was inhuman. Islands, breaks and bars certainly do indicate troubles but some of the other markings can be very helpful.

## The Heart Line in Sections (Fig. 7.33)

The heart line can be divided into three sections as follows:

a) Heart line of the affections.
b) Love and sensitivity.
c) Heart and lungs.

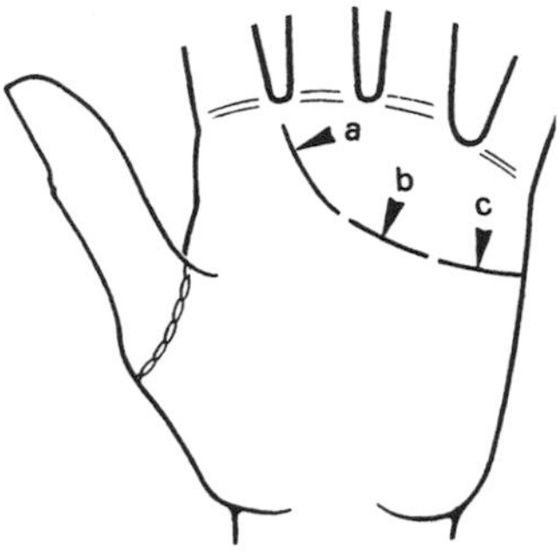

There are health indications to be seen on the heart line as a whole, but section c) is mainly concerned with health.

Figure 7.33

## Where Does the Heart Line Begin?

Palmists and palmistry books disagree on the starting point for the heart line, but we have decided to settle on calling the percussion edge the starting point. This is because the head and life line both start at their thickest point so it makes sense for the heart line to do so too. Events cannot really be dated by their position on the heart line, so if you see a trauma mark on the heart line please check the fate, Apollo and life lines, and even the head line for corroboration and dating.

## Heart Line of the Affections

This part of the heart line is on the radial, active part of the hand. It is how we give and receive love and it shows our attitude to sex and the part it plays in our lives, including the way we show and express ourselves to others and to the outside world. It might be a good idea to think of that part of the line as a hand reaching out for affection. Branches bring more feeling and receptivity—few branches mean pre-set views. A single line signifies single-mindedness while many lines suggest a reaching out and searching for something which may not exist.

Look at the quality of the line. A wispy line, barely on the skin, shows little emotional or sexual fulfillment, and a dark patch of skin

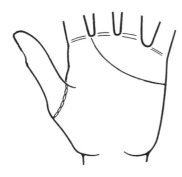

Figure 7.34

under the line shows anguish or depression over the emotional side of life.

## Curved Heart Line (Fig. 7.34)

Looking at the heart line as a whole for the moment, curved lines show emotion while a straight line indicates control. A curved heart line belongs to a person who wants to relate because he is warmhearted and highly sexual. A combination of a long, curved heart line and head line shows a good memory for emotional matters. This person will remember both the good times and the pain of past emotional experiences. Curved line people are more open emotionally; they do not expect to find envy, spite or domination in a relationship, and they do not set out deliberately to hurt others.

This person is a good communicator who will argue, cry, express affection and show his feelings. If a relationship ends, he will become openly upset, even hysterical, and will be willing to talk about his feelings, but in due course, he will move on to make a new relationship with someone new.

## Straight Heart Line (Fig. 7.35)

This person is emotionally controlled. If the line is exceptionally straight, he may seek perfection in relationships. He operates well on a level of friendship but less so in close personal relationships because he becomes upset if confronted with deep feelings. He complains that his partner does not care enough for him but he keeps his lover at arm's length—possibly without quite realizing it.

This subject is a poor communicator who says little and may punish his partner with silences when he feels put out. Unfortunately, he will do this

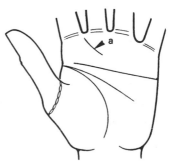

Figure 7.35

even if he has become upset by something outside the home that has absolutely nothing to do with the partner and that the partner isn't even aware of.

If a relationship ends, he will say little but will brood and allow his feelings to go inwards and to fester. He may find it hard to move on to someone new with any kind of trust or optimism. A straight heart line that has an extra piece above is a combination of both types. This person is cautious and inclined to hide his feelings, but later in life he develops the courage to express his feelings both to show his affection and to complain when hurt.

## Straight Heart Line with a Whole or Partial Girdle of Venus (Fig. 7.35)

Quite often one sees a straight line with all or part of the girdle of Venus above it (see chapter nine). This adds sensitivity. This person may fence off his feelings in order to protect them. At least he can feel his own pain, even if he still has trouble relating to the pain of others, so he has the potential to become warmer-hearted and a better lover.

## Straight Heart Line Ending on Lower Jupiter (Fig. 7.36a)

This shows a "mental" type of loving. This person needs to feel proud of his partner. He may love her because she looks right, because she has the right career or position in life, because she comes from the right religious group, family group or class and due to her financial prospects. Having chosen an acceptable mate, he proceeds to fantasize about what love could and should be like—if only in his dreams. This is even more likely if there is a long, curved head line.

The heart line in this position can have an interesting practical application in that this person will have a very caring attitude toward people

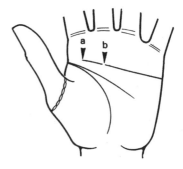

Figure 7.36

who are outside the immediate family. The sexual energy and expression is frequently expended in the career. These subjects often choose careers in nursing, teaching and social work, particularly if they have healing or medical striata. Someone with a straight heart line does not need a constant display of affection. Our friend Sheila McGuirk has noticed that these people are frequently seen to have a strongly marked Solomon's ring or caring line, which seems to imply that they are happiest when expressing love in a practical way for the community as a whole, while feeling less comfortable in personal relationships. This kind of formation is also seen on the hands of paternal businessmen who look after the interests of their staff.

## Straight Heart Line Ending Under Saturn (Fig. 7.36b)

This short heart line belongs to a person who can withdraw into himself. When Malcolm was in America he saw a lady in her sixties who had a heart line like this and he suggested that although she had been married three times she said that she didn't know what love really is. This heart line can only cope with a mental type of love or sex with no real feeling. In a woman's hand there is a shrewd calculated approach to relationships where all the emotions and sexual expression are held back for fear of ridicule or rejection.

## Curved Heart Line Ending Under Saturn (Fig. 7.37)

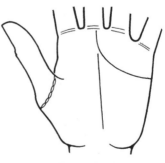

Figure 7.37

This line goes back to the self, so it displays a selfish outlook. The person is cold, not easily carried away emotionally and the emotions are governed by sensuality. If the fate line joins the heart line, the subject's heart may be poured into his work or pastimes. There may be a stifling of romantic and sexual feelings possibly caused by hidden gay needs. A cheerful person who has no problem with his or

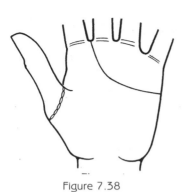

Figure 7.38

her sexuality has an ordinary looking heart line. If there has been pressure from parents on the subject of gayness, there may be a scimitar-shaped hook downward into the area where the head and life line join.

## Heart Line Ending Between Jupiter and Saturn (Fig. 7.38)

If this line is single with few branches and no chaining but with a vigorous curve, the sexual energy flows freely, therefore it is physical, instinctive, passionate and demanding. There may be a selfish attitude to sex with little discussion of mutual needs, because the subject considers that actions speak louder than words.

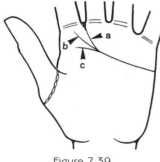

Figure 7.39

## Ending Between Jupiter and Saturn, but with a Gentle Curve (Fig. 7.39a)

A line like this with branches refers to a warm heart and balance between the mind and the emotions. If the line travels tightly upwards between the fingers, the subject will see no wrong in the partner. If the heart line ends in a single line, there could be a single-minded attitude. The subject may be possessive or idealistic about relationships.

## Heart Line Ending on Jupiter (Fig. 7.39b)

This is where the character of the mount of Jupiter comes into play. There is idealism, ambition and egotism. If the heart line touches the base of the finger there will be jealousy and possessiveness. If the line is strong, single and gently curved the subject may boast about his sexual conquests—but the activities take place mainly in his imagination. He wants to make love without a hair out of place and he needs to keep his wristwatch on so that he does not feel totally denuded. If he cannot unbend, the sexual energy goes into ambition, especially if the fate line goes into the heart line and if there is also a strong Jupiter finger. If there is a branch line going into the lower part of Jupiter, (b and c) the person will be more open and down-to-earth, and he will have a more caring attitude to others.

## Branch Lines Flowing Toward the Junction of the Head and Life Lines

This kind of branch may be curved or rather straight. It means that the subject is extremely cautious when it comes to relating. He is reluctant to let go and give his love freely. There may be complex reasons that reach back into his childhood. He may have had his love thrown back into his face or he may have been abused. Even if things were not that bad, something wasn't quite right. Homosexual hands are no different from heterosexual ones, except in those cases where the subject perceives his sexuality to be a problem.

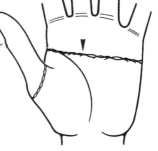

## The Simian Line (Fig. 7.40)

We have already dealt with this in the section on the head line but we would like to mention it here in connection with the feelings and emotions.

These people can only concentrate on one thing at a time so there is a tendency to be overbearing. They

Figure 7.40

enter wholeheartedly into whatever they do and switch off all else. When it comes to love and the emotions, this single-mindedness is hard to live with unless one enters the relationship with the same intensity. It is hard for a person with this line to understand the feelings of others. They can swamp their partner with love that may be born of insecurity and lack of confidence. They can be very possessive, jealous and even violent. Sometimes they feel love is a sign of weakness.

If the subject is aware of his nature and tries to become more receptive to others, another heart line will begin to develop, probably a partial line as a curve under Jupiter and Saturn, and this will put him in touch with both his own feelings and those of others. Sometimes the girdle of Venus becomes strong enough to be an infant heart line, and this serves the purpose.

## Semi-Simians and Other Unusual Lines (Figs. 7.41 and 7.42)

Semi-simian lines show social or sexual hang-ups. These people are either so shy that they find it hard to talk personally to anyone or they may suffer from some form of sexual confusion. There may be other fears and phobias related to childhood experiences. Sometimes subjects with these lines find it difficult to feel and to express affection in the usual manner. They may be so involved with their per-

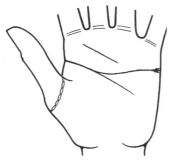

Figure 7.41

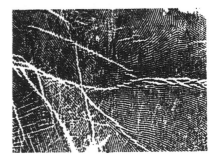

Figure 7.42

sonal image, in love with their car, their property or their bank account, that they cannot relate to people. Others have a strong sex drive, but outside the confines of the bedroom are unwilling and unable to cope with a relationship.

## Center Section of the Heart Line (Fig. 7.43)

This section concerns sensitivity, and it is apt to change its appearance very quickly because it reacts to the subject's feelings at any one time.

*(Fig. 7.43a)*
If there is a single heart line with no branches, the subject will keep a tight hold on his emotions and want to be in control or to avoid being hurt. This subject finds it hard to understand that it takes two to make a relationship, although he can be loyal to his chosen partner. Emotional difficulty or a shock shows up as an island or a number of islands in the central section of the line.

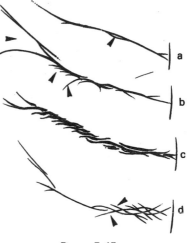

Figure 7.43

*(Fig. 7.43b)*
This is the same type of line as above but more sensitive, volatile and insecure. This person experiences ups and downs and hurts in emotions. Short, curved branches falling below the line are flirtation lines. Long, downward-curved branches represent emotional disappointments. Branches at the affection end of the heart line give warmth and idealism, passion and a sensible approach to relationships and to other people. This is the area where you find friendships. A couple of strong lines curving downwards here show deep abiding friendships.

*(Fig. 7.43c)*
A woven type of heart line shows sensitivity brought about by mineral deficiencies in the diet. This can also show depression. The subject needs to calm down because he or she is hypersensitive.

*(Fig. 743d)*
Look at this heart line in its entirety but only at the sensitivity aspect. Here we have a spiky thorny looking line under Mercury. When the spikes face inwards toward the palm, the subjects are emotionally spiky. They may fight the world as though they were still fighting tough battles left over from their childhood. They may even persecute themselves.

*(Fig. 7.44)*
A break in the line just where it begins to curve upwards (a) seems to show the sudden ending of a relationship. This may be due to sud-

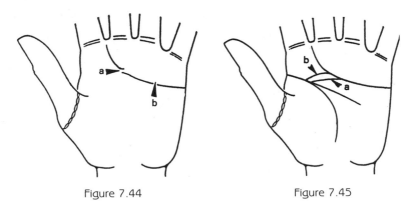

| Figure 7.44 | Figure 7.45 |

den divorce or death. Look also for a deletion line near the end of an attachment line, plus a spinster line. If there is an isolated island on this section, the spouse might be seriously ill. If the line continues cleanly after the island and/or there is an effort line rising up from the heart line, the spouse will recover completely. The late palmist John Lindsay told us that a clean break between the Mercury and Apollo area (b) shows celibacy—as in the case of a Catholic priest. Sometimes the person loves one person but has sex with another.

## Lines that Firmly Join the Heart Line to the Head Line (Fig. 7.45)

A line that firmly joins the heart line to the head line (a *or* b) shows a marriage of non-communication. If there are two of these (a *and* b), the subject may have left one non-relater only to find another!

## Double Heart Lines (Fig. 7.46)

(a) These are supposed to be a sign of deep loyalty. They suggest an amorous nature and tremendous devotion in love. An extra line here strengthens the heart line in the same way that the line of Mars

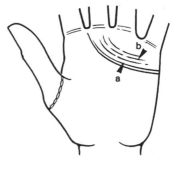

Figure 7.46

aids the life line. Double heart lines also make for a lively and animated personality.

(b) A shadow of the heart line, with fragments repeated above the line, show some form of other loy-
alty. We have seen this in the case of people who have remarried and have almost completely cut them-selves off from their previous fam-ily, but there are lingering feelings for the children.

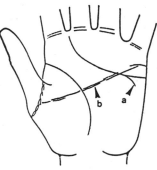

## Influence Lines (Fig. 7.47)

Those that join the heart line from beneath the heart line (a) signify use-ful friendships, friends in high places

Figure 7.47

or good business associations. Those that creep over from within the life line show that relatives or in-laws make trouble for the person and partner.

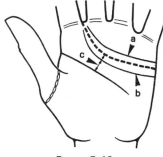

Figure 7.48

## Determining the Position of the Line (Fig. 7.48)

If the heart line is close to the fingers (a) it suggests an intellectual approach to love, along with a rational and cool attitude. In this case, the head rules the heart. A deeply curved line that is low on the palm (b), and if there are pudgy mounts, signifies a person who pours out love to help others. A gradual curve shows that the heart rules the head, and even more so if there is a star mark near the end of the head line or on Luna. When the heart line is close to the head line (c), the person is narrow-minded.

It is also worth noting that people who have curved heart lines are more domesticated and home-loving on the whole than the people with straight lines, who are probably more career-minded.

## Other Marks

Crosses and bars are setbacks and interference of some kind. Discolored, faded, smudgy, whitish or glassy patches show periods of trouble, illness or depression over personal relationships. These will clear up as the problem passes away.

## Examples of Real Heart Lines

### Karen—detached heart line (Fig. 7.49)

Figure 7.49

The first impression given by this line makes one think of heart trouble because the line stops short on the ulna side of the hand, but the lower semi-simian line acts as a replacement for the missing part of the heart line. This type of line is found on the hands of warm-hearted people and the humor loop resting on this line makes this attractive young lady delightful to be with. The doubled heart line indicates loyalty, while the semi-simian indicates shyness. This young woman desperately wants a boyfriend but is unable to overcome her reserve. This is typical of people who are unsure of themselves sexually and unsure of exactly what they need and how to get it. They are happy to relate as a friend but find the emotional side nerve-racking. They need a loving, caring partner.

### Jackie—girdle of Venus pushing down the heart line (Fig. 7.50)

Figure 7.50

In this hand, all the major lines are chained, making the subject feel as if she herself is in chains. The amount of emotional energy produced in this person's body is more than the head line can cope

Figure 7.51            Figure 7.52

with. At the age of sixteen she showed a tendency toward hysteria, depression and nymphomania. She has since spent her life in and out of institutions.

### Jason—straight heart line (Fig. 7.51)
This is not a simian line because of the separate head line. A little embryo heart line gives a certain balance.

### Terry—straight and tight line (Fig. 7.52)
Terry is a businessman whose wife died in an accident in a car that he was driving. Note the island in the sensitive section of the heart line indicating a terrible emotional shock. The relationship lines on Venus stop at the age point when the accident occurred and a dot marks the place.

## Doubled lines

These show split energies according to the line involved. Double fate or head line shows there could be two parallel careers. If the heart line is doubled, there could be a peculiar way of relating to others or a tendency to blow hot and cold. A doubled life line suggests there could be two separate issues that take up the subject's time. The idea behind this doubling is either that of double duties or of a split personality.

# CHAPTER EIGHT

# A NEW WAY OF LOOKING AT LINES

This is where our book differs radically from previous hand-reading books. We have already introduced the reader to new concepts, such as realistic hand shapes and energy rhythms, but the following drawings and ideas are so different that they may appear confusing at first glance. We suggest that you take this section bit by bit, taking a long look at your friends' hands and checking their experiences against our findings until you feel completely at home with our concepts.

We would like to see our readers looking at the hand as a whole rather than taking a line-by-line analysis. We want you to be like an art critic studying a new painting, who first looks at the whole picture and then examines it in block segments. It may look complicated, but you will soon get the hang of it!

## How to Read Events in the Hand

This section brings together all the previous chapters because while you are reading from one area of the hand, you will need to modify your conclusions by constant reference to other characteristics on the hand. For instance, if there is strong evidence that your subject will need to care for sick or elderly parents, take into consideration whether he has the type of personality capable of doing this. Positive indications would be a rounded (conic) hand, a line of Solomon, "waisted" thumbs and fingers, curving heart line, sloping head line, fingers that space slightly and Jupiter finger curving slightly towards Saturn. Negative indications would be a heavy square hand with whorls on the fingers, a Jupiter finger that bends sharply outwards, a heavy thumb, a straight head line and high mounts of Venus, Jupiter and Mars. This subject would get his partner to do it!

Remember that the dominant hand is reality, while the minor hand is the "1 wish" hand. All this is going to take practice but it has a logical basis, even if it appears a little obscure at first. Just remember this simple rule: vertical lines that travel toward the radial side indicate improvement, motivation and action. Lines that travel toward the ulna side show inner achievement, homely pleasures and successes—and sometimes setbacks if on the fate line.

It is essential to bear in mind the meaning and characteristic of each line and the direction it is taking. Remember the meaning of the mounts or areas of the hand. We have divided the hand into three horizontal zones which, for clarity, we have termed lower, middle and upper zone, and we have started our analysis at the lower zone.

## Lower Zone—Childhood to Aproximately Thirty to Thirty-Five Years

The earliest experiences of life are drawn deeply into the psyche and can affect our behavior and motivation ever after. We are all familiar with the type of person who, having been brought up in extreme poverty, fights his way to success and riches. How much of this ambition is part of his nature and how much of it is due to his early environment? This is the crux of the "nature or nurture" argument and also Jung's theory of the collective unconscious and unconscious ancestral memories.

## Lower Zone—Life Line Arching Outwards into the Palm (Fig. 8.1a)

When the line is continuous and it arcs outwards toward the palm, there is a balance between the inner needs and worldly achievement. These people need love and family life as well as a career. They have a reasonably adventurous nature. They enjoy travel, meeting new people and take an interest in the world about them. They seek a secure and sensible home life and probably want more for themselves and their children than their parents were able to provide.

## Life Line Clinging Around Venus (Fig. 8.1b)

This person needs *inner* satisfaction. He is a good relater and he needs a partner to love. Work is secondary unless it gives strong *inner* satisfaction, such as art, music and craftsmanship. Not being very adventurous, he gains most of his pleasures from quite homely

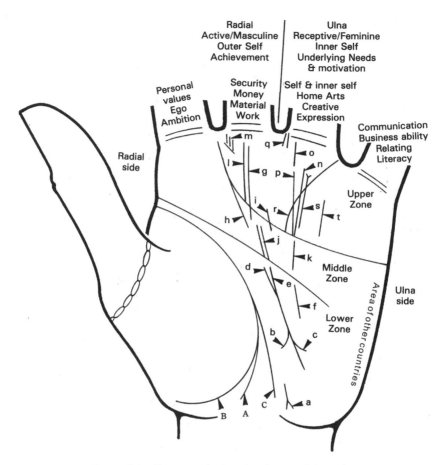

Figure 8.1  Events in the hand and map of the palm

pursuits, so he may have a beautiful garden. He either wants to repeat the kind of home life his parents provided or just falls into their way of doing things.

## Life Line Reaching out into Luna (Fig. 8.1c)

Eventually work will become more important to this subject than home—even if he works from his home. He will put his energies into getting on. His spirit is adventurous and he may feel stifled by domestic matters. He is interested in the world outside and will want to leave an impression on it. He will strive for a better or different standard of living from that of his parents and may move geographically a long distance from the place of his birth. If there is no great geographic move, then look for a dramatic difference in aspirations.

A wife may develop a totally different outlook from her husband during the course of marriage, especially if the marriage took place early in life. There could be a strong reaction against childhood poverty or against the kind of marriage that contains nothing other than talk about the home and children.

## Life Line Splitting at the Southern End (Fig. 7.2)

The subject's energies are split. This could be a medical condition (check with upper zone and our chapter on health). There could be a split in the subject's inner needs that fluctuate between wanting to concentrate on the emotional side and the career side of life. When the life line is split although the two forks are close together and with no fate line on the lower zone, life is seen as a struggle, it is a matter of survival. A typical case would be that of a single parent.

## Fate Line—Lower Zone

When reading the fate line in this zone, the nearby life line represents the parents and home.

## No Fate Line

The subject has no particular ambition at this stage. Powerful parents may dominate him or life may be too comfortable at home for him to want to strike out on his own. He may drift along or live in a protected environment such as the services, or even in some kind of prison. If there is mental illness, there might be a brownish stain on the skin. This person is not a self-starter during his youth, and he might have to wait for his courage to develop or for a change of circumstances to stir him into action.

## Fate Line Part of the Life Line

First check that this is not a split life line, which has a different meaning. This registers a restricted early life, this subject may be held back by his parents or he could work in the family business. This could turn out to be a useful start for him if he develops ambition later on. A long or thick Jupiter finger and a strong-looking thumb would provide an instant clue. Even though this might hamper him, he could be grateful for a job when jobs are hard to find—having a fate line implies at least some sense of responsibility.

## Fate Line Starts Separate from the Life Line

This shows independence and leaving home early. If there are lines connecting the fate line to the life line, the subject will keep in touch with his parents and will return from time to time. The greater the distance between the fate and life lines, the greater the distance mentally and physically, from the parental home. This is an independent and self-reliant young person. A line that breaks and overlaps on the ulna side means that the subject will move away from his childhood hometown.

## Fate Line Beginning on the Inside of the Life Line, on the Mount of Venus

His family dictates to this person. They rule his career and personal life, and he is unable to liberate himself. Perhaps he prefers it that way.

## Lines That Run Into and Join the Fate Line (Fig. 8.1)

a   A subject with a joining line or lines very low down on the palm will be physically and mentally ready for a serious relationship when still very young. The point at which the line enters the fate line can determine the age. If a subject marries at some age before there are any joining lines, he may not be ready for such a relationship and this could cause problems later.

b   A line that enters the fate line from the radial side indicates meeting a partner through work or through one's parents.

c A line entering from the ulna side shows that the partner is chosen from the world outside and away from the influence of parents and co-workers. This person makes an impression on people outside the family and looks for work that offers changes of scenery. A long line entering the fate line indicates an important early relationship. The hands, of course, only register emotional commitment and not ceremonies or certificates. A fine line from the ulna side could indicate help and training at work.

## No Lines Entering the Fate Line

It is quite possible for a person to be married with no lines entering the fate line. The marriage will be for convenience, a suitable arrangement all around—love, it is hoped, will come later.

## Y-Shaped Split in the Fate Line

This amazingly common mark indicates a change of direction and a fresh start. This might relate to the home, career, job, relationship or anything.

*(Fig. 8.1d)*
If the split line on the radial side stops, the material and career side of life will take a back seat while the domestic and emotional side develop, such as when a young woman gives up work to have children.

*(Fig. 8.1e)*
If the branch line on the ulna side stops, career, money and ambition will become important while the emotional side is left for the time being.

## No Apollo Line

The subject doesn't have a home of his own or he could be moving around in connection with his job, living in rented accommodation and not yet settled in a permanent place.

## Clear Apollo Line (Fig. 8.1f)

The home should be well established early in life. The subject could make a profession in the arts or he could have a strong attachment to the area he grew up in.

## Two Fate Lines

Life seems to be out of phase and the person wishes that he had gone down a different road when it was open to him than the one that he has gone down. There is an element of regret.

## Case History: Janet (lower zone) (Fig. 8.2)

- Janet married at nineteen (a). The marriage was full of difficulties, hence the series of islands.
- The large island shows the couple trying to come together. Notice the lines (b) nearly touching, also a line entering the fate line (f) signifying a coming together.
- Janet went back to her parents (c). Here the life line is used to represent the parents. At the same time the split (d), a decision line cutting across, in addition to an island on the life line, shows a period of depression and unhappiness.

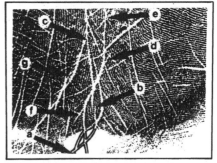

Figure 8.2

- She will meet another man at age twenty-four to twenty-five, when a line (e) enters the fate line and pushes the route of the fate line toward Jupiter. Also the influence lines stop at twenty-five, so life becomes easier and she begins to take control of her own life.

## Middle Zone

Age approximately between thirty to thirty-five and forty to forty-five years.

## Fate Line (Fig. 8.1g)

If it is travelling towards Saturn, work is for money and not for job satisfaction.

*(Fig. 8.1h)*
If the fate line joins the heart line, the heart will be put into work. A fate line that runs into the girdle of Venus means a workaholic.

*(Fig. 8.1i)*
The extra short line between the fate and Apollo lines indicates starting a business or working from home.

*(Fig. 8.1j)*
Where there are two parallel lines the person's energy is used to the full. The subject is fully stretched and he is taking on too much. This could be due to running a small business or some kind of freelance work. Incidentally, this is a good indication on a young woman's hand that she will have children, as the pressure on her time and energy can be greatest when working and bringing up children. (Other indications of motherhood are small lines falling away from the life line on the mount of Venus side, possibly due to the physical strain of pregnancy; also children lines—see Chapter 9.)

## Apollo Line (Fig. 8.1k)

Note how the lines begin to spread themselves outwards in this part of the hand. An Apollo line in this area indicates an emphasis on home, relationships and inner needs. If the Apollo line jumps, branches or leans to the ulna side the domestic and emotional side of life will be even more emphasized.

If the Apollo line seems to draw fine lines away from the fate line in this area, the subject could work from home or search strongly for self-expression and inner satisfaction in his work. This would point to the need for a creative outlet.

The meaning of some of the findings in the upper zone can relate to middle zone matters. For instance, a person could start a business at any age, but this may only show in the upper zone.

## Y-Shaped Split on Apollo

Same as per the fate line.

## Case History: Thomas (middle zone) (Fig. 8.3)

Thomas is now forty-three and this story started when he was twenty-nine, so some of the earlier fine lines are now breaking up and fading.

- An islanded interference line (a) crosses the life line, cuts into the fate and Apollo lines and ends in a wart (b). All this, especially the wart, indicates a time of great stress.
- An island on the fate line (c) shows that this period of stress affected the whole of his life at that time.
- Thomas married at the age of twenty-nine, and later on had casual affair with a woman he met at work. Note that at the beginning of the island (c), the lines run parallel. The closeness and then converging of the tiny line *inside* the island (d), coming from the ulna

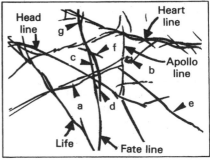

Figure 8.3

side but *inside* the island to touch the radial side, would indicate an affair with someone at work.

- His in-laws got to hear of the affair, and forced him to act—note the decision line (a). This line is found on many hands and can be traced from the family line across the hand to just under the attachment lines on the ulna side. It shows marriage difficulties and interference by parents or in-laws. Indeed they may be the cause of the difficulties.

- In order to prevent a full-scale scandal, Thomas's company decided to send him to work in their German branch (e). The split or extra head line travels outwards from the main influence line and the wart (b). Nature tends to grab the nearest line and utilize it in order to tell its story. As this line (e) goes to the area of travel and other countries at one end and stops at the interference line at the other with a long island (c), one can only deduce that his trip to Germany gave him time and space to think things out.

- If you extend this line (e) upward to the fate line, it becomes another decision line (f). The couple come together here for a few years and then finally separate at the split (g) just under the heart line, when Thomas was thirty-eight.

## Upper Zone

Life from ages approximately forty to forty-five onwards. This zone is most important because the findings here can be projected back to the other two zones, as the lifestyle projected here has its roots in the events of the lower two zones.

## Lack of Lines

On an empty hand one must search carefully for lines under the skin. If there is a blank area above the fate and Apollo lines, there will be a drop in the energies. This subject could become ill or just give up on life, allowing a kind of lethargy to set in. One must look for medical problems that may show up on the life and heart lines. On a more mundane level, there may be financial loss or the loss of a relationship that causes material and emotional hardship.

# Fate Line (Fig. 8.1g)

One fate line traveling towards Saturn shows single mindedness or a secure and unchanging life. This person would stay in the same job for years and he might receive a secure and regular income. A fine supplementary line on the ulna side of the fate line indicates a supplementary income, perhaps from a second job.

# Two Parallel Lines (Fig. 8.1g and l)

These suggest freelance work, self-employment, having to turn one's hands to anything, or struggling with a very difficult job and a lot of responsibility.

# Many Strong Lines

Many lines around the fate line indicate that finances are being stretched. If there is a large blank area to the north, the subject may overdo things and develop health problems as a result. Another outcome may be that he cannot win the battle against mounting losses and finds himself broke, bankrupt, etc. A secondary fate line going toward Apollo shows a new kind of job that would be based in or around the home. A secondary fate line that reaches toward the Apollo finger shows inherited money or money from family sources.

# Many Fine Lines (Fig. 8.1m)

This could indicate a drinking or drug problem. The subject may just be searching for a better way of life or he could be a dabbler in business, a generally inconsistent type of person. This could indicate lending money to others or keeping busy in old age or both.

# Apollo Line (Fig. 8.1n)

It is sometimes rather difficult to establish which line actually *is* the Apollo line here. It might be a good idea to push the hand away from you a bit in order to see which line stands out most. Note which line is the deepest or least broken up. Once you have established the Apollo line, take it to represent the subject's home base. If the line reaches well down into the middle zone, he would live in the same area, probably the same house, for many years. If the line suddenly fades out and there is a blank area to the north, the subject could lose his home and possessions through financial disaster or marriage difficulties.

## New Lines (Fig. 8.1o)

Lines that start again after a break indicate a new home, a move or a fresh start, probably rather late in life. An island on this line means problems and troubles connected with property matters or even living in a jinxed or unlucky house.

## Y Shape at the Top of the Apollo Line

A large split here means living with a difficult person and a small split denotes living with someone whose health is poor or who is disabled or incapacitated. The partner or parent requires extra help and attention but manages to lead as normal a life as possible with plenty of activities.

## Split Apollo Line (Fig. 8.1p)

This signifies a couple living together side by side with separate interests, co-existing rather than making a true relationship. A big split that starts at the heart line and forms a slight hollow between the two splitting lines means the partner has a long-term disability. Look also for a close split at the southern end of the life line.

## Lines on the Radial Side of Apollo (Fig. 8.1p)

Fine lines that are almost parallel indicate a wish to move house that is *not* fulfilled. If the lines become stronger, the move may then take place. A line that merges with Apollo may indicate a second home that has been purchased as an investment.

## Two Parallel Lines at the Top of Apollo (Fig. 8.1q)

This means living with someone in old age, possibly family or a friend. If the two lines lean toward one another or merge, this will be a love relationship. The lower end of the life line will also curve around the mount of Venus.

## Lines on the Radial Side of Apollo (Fig. 8.1r)

These refer to hobbies, studies, work in the arts or work at home. This can also show that the subject works in or near the home in a counseling or healing capacity.

If the line reaches over toward the Mercury finger, it indicates that the subject is actively seeking out people with like minds—those who are on his wavelength. This can have a bearing on current and future relationships, because these people develop interests that become part of themselves, and which lead them to associate with similar people.

These subjects may move ahead intellectually, socially or spiritually so quickly that they finally discover that they have very little in common with their long-term partner. A line here that is close to Apollo can also indicate a person who works with animals.

## Lines on the Ulna Side of Apollo (Fig. 8.1s)

This side of Apollo concerns those who are closely connected with the subject. The closer the lines are to Apollo, the closer the connection, while the further away the greater the distance, either geographical or emotional. In this area of the hand one will find parents who need help. These subjects would look after parents until the end of their days. If there is a small blocking line where the line terminates, this is also the death of a loved one. However, if the line splits at the top, the person being taken care of will be disabled or incapacitated.

Another meaning to the same kind of line may be a close sexual relationship, possibly in addition to the marriage. Yet another is that mother might come to tea and stay for years! Either way it means that the subject has to put himself out for someone else, and that he may actually be very happy to do so. A Y formation here shows an unhappy relationship. It can also show that the subject's affections are poured into caring for animals.

## Line Parallel to Apollo (Fig. 8.1t)

This outpost of Apollo shows love and duty at a distance. It may mean that the subject worries about his parents or some other person who lives at a distance. It could show life in two homes. To check this, look to see if there are also two family lines at the appropriate age of the placement. The person may long to put distance between himself and his family, if they make him miserable, or he could long to escape responsibilities. If these lines join, there may be a marriage to a friend who lives far away.

## Case History: Samuel, a Retired Farmer (Fig. 8.4)

This print belongs to Sam, who is now aged sixty-three. He comes from a farming family and is himself a farmer.

- Sam began his career by working for his father, as shown by the fate line inside the life line (a).
- At approximately the age of twenty-three he got his own farm. He had wished to be independent for a long time. The fate line that is hidden below the level of the skin before that age shows this urge.
- At the age of twenty-four he married (b). The fate line becomes stronger here and the two lines coming together show a union. There was an element of social pressure because it was correct to marry and have sons to carry on the tradition of the land. His wife is also shown on Venus (c), with a line forming from the family line showing a decision.
- An effort line (d) with an island shows illness—in this case, lung trouble. (An island under Mercury or under the Apollo and Mercury junction denotes heart or lung problems.) This meant that it took considerable effort for him to get his farm going.
- In his thirties the fate line travels toward Jupiter showing an improvement in his business.
- When Sam was in his forties his father was becoming too frail to cope with farming, so he asked Sam to help out on the parental farm. A line from the family line shows that he had to alter his life. The line on the radial side of the Apollo line shows him helping his father.

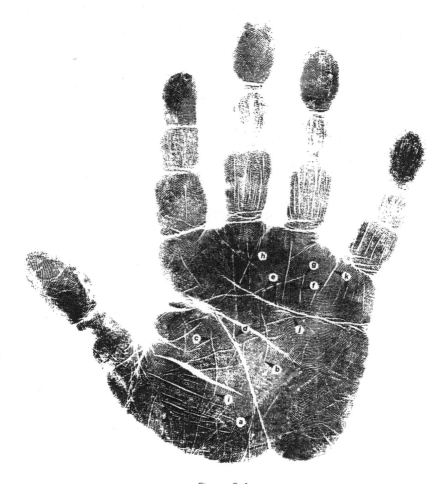

Figure 8.4

- The line representing his parents ends when his father dies. Sam is now forty-six years of age. He helped his mother to keep the farm going until she died when Sam was fifty-two years old.
- The line (h) running from the family line where the two fate lines cross pictures him bringing the two farms together into one unit. The line to Apollo also shows a legacy.
- His wife died when he was sixty-one years of age. Note how the line on Venus becomes light, also the shock island on the heart line. There is even a line from his marriage on Venus to this

island. Now the lines are delving under the skin as he passes his farm on to his son.

- Note also the strong teaching line and healing lines (k). He has always worked with cattle rather than cereals, using his ability to heal and care for living creatures. The teaching line shows that he is able to judge cattle at shows. Now that he has retired, this is his main interest in life.

# CHAPTER NINE

# THE RELATING LINES

We call the small strong horizontal lines that enter the hand from the percussion side of the mount of Mercury "attachment lines" because nowadays many people choose to live together without actually marrying. These lines give the palmist a good deal of information about the subject's attitude of mind (and body) to strong and close long-term emotional relationships.

## One Strong Line

All being well, this should indicate one steady marriage-type relationship. If the line is bold and clear and the heart line is also clean and clear, this subject should enjoy a long and happy marriage. It is a real pleasure to see a hand like this as it is all too rare. This person marries with the intention of being totally faithful in body and loyal in mind to his partner. There is a supportive attitude to the spouse, and the subject has the ability to overlook the occasional outburst or aggravating mood. There is little likelihood of this kind of marriage ending, but in the event of this occurring, the subject would marry again with the same intention of steady faithfulness.

From time to time we see this kind of hand on an elderly widow, and when we suggest that the marriage was a happy one, she agrees and may even be seen wiping away a tear or two. These elderly people truly miss their companion, and they rarely remarry but stay faithful to their partner's memory.

## Two Strong Lines

These subjects usually marry more than once. This could be because they do not find the right partner the first time around, or question themselves as to the type of marriage they want and then decide against the one that they have. If their partner leaves them, they usually marry again.

## Three or More Lines

These people like relationships but need sexual freedom. This is especially true if there is a girdle of Venus that reaches across the hand to the mount of Mercury. This would make any really long-term relationship impossible unless there was a strong financial reason for it.

Sometimes these lines indicate a period of dating, experimenting and looking around, which may be due to the youth of the subject or perhaps one of those periods that can occur after a divorce or between times. Once the person settles down again, the lighter extra lines fade away, leaving one or two strong lines on the hand.

## Strength of Feelings

Look on the percussion side of the hand toward the back of the hand. If there is one line or one major one that appears to be made up of two lines that converge to make one attachment line, the feelings for the partner are very strong. If the lines don't join, there may be other reasons for the marriage or it may have been entered into rather lightly.

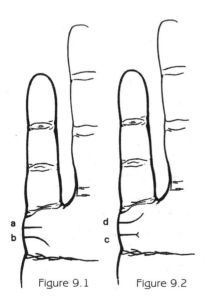

Figure 9.1     Figure 9.2

## One Straight Line (Fig. 9.1a)

This indicates one good marriage.

## A Line That Curves down (Fig. 9.1b)

This shows disappointment that can lead to parting or divorce. The subject feels himself to be dominated or put upon by the partner and he may have to tolerate rather miserable circumstances in order to keep the peace.

## A Straight Line with a Small Fork (Fig. 9.2c)

This signifies a sudden decision to end the marriage. A client of ours who had struggled through sixteen years of a really rotten marriage once said to us, "One day a bell seemed to ring somewhere in my head and I took myself off to see a solicitor. After discussing the formalities he asked me if I had any second thoughts. I found myself replying that I wished that I had had the courage to do this many years before."

If practically the whole line is forked the subject is aware, albeit unconsciously, that the marriage has never been fulfilling. This can still lead to divorce but in a more leisurely fashion, perhaps when the children are grown up or there is enough money in the kitty to comfortably support two homes.

## A Line That Curves Upwards (Fig. 9.2d)

A line that can be seen curving upwards shows that the subject has a partner who will do well in the world. The improvement in the spouse's income and status could be of great benefit to the subject. If this is the case, the heart line will be clean and clear, the fate line smooth and aiming toward Jupiter, there will be an isolated cross high on Jupiter and there will be no other strongly-marked attachment lines.

However, human nature being what it is, there can be friction and jealousy due to the change in their situation—especially if it is the woman who does well. If it is the man who does well, he may find the wife who helped him to reach his elevated position now appears too plain and suburban for his new lifestyle. There is no guarantee that this will lead to divorce, but if there are gaps and changes of direction in the heart line there is a strong indication that the marriage will not stand the changed circumstances.

## Branch Curving Upwards (Fig. 9.3e)

If there is a small line that branches upwards from the attachment line, the case is similar to the attachment line itself curving upwards but not so drastic. The partner will be successful, but this should not be particularly stressful to the marriage. Alternatively, this may show a successful hobby or interest for the partner.

## Bubble on an Attachment Line (Fig. 9.3f)

An island or bubble on an attachment line indicates that the partner will be very ill or have some desperate problem to overcome. This kind of mark may appear at the time of trouble and slip away again some time later.

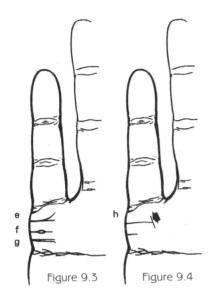

e
f
g

Figure 9.3   Figure 9.4

h

## Parallel Lines (Fig. 9.3g)

The partners coexist for years but the marriage is not emotionally close or satisfying.

## Deletion Line (Fig. 9.4h)

We call this a deletion line because it often appears when a marriage is breaking up. The deletion line vanishes again when the fuss is all over. The new line seems to mark an end to the marriage, just like a correction in a line of writing. Those who are accustomed to looking at their hands may notice this for themselves, and in some cases make the connection with what is going on.

## Widowhood Line (Fig. 9.5j)

Sometimes this is called the spinster line (this must be clear and unbroken). It is as if these people should never be married at all, because their mates usually die suddenly. Malcolm has seen this line in a woman who has lost three husbands.

Sasha noticed this line forming over a period of two or three years and her husband, Tony, died. She met Jan and remarried, and she is glad to report that the widowhood line has vanished from her hand.

j

Figure 9.5

## Companion Lines (Fig. 9.6)

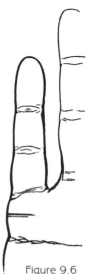

These exceptionally fine lines that accompany the attachment line indicate that the subject is not completely fulfilled by marriage alone however close and apparently successful the relationship. The subject may be deeply committed to an interesting career or a fascinating hobby.

In some cases there will be a need for affairs or other relationships on the side. The reason for this could just possibly be figured out from the way that the heart line curves. If it curves up toward the Jupiter finger, but with the line weakening and softening toward the end, this could imply that the marriage, although good in many ways, leaves the subject sexually unfulfilled.

Sasha once had to demonstrate hand reading at a college seminar. The vice-headmaster of the college enthusiastically offered a print of his hand for the

Figure 9.6

occasion. Sasha put the print onto a transparency and used an overhead projector. She carefully went through all the various lines and marks on his hand, much to the surprise of the assembled company, who had no idea that a skilled palmist could see so much on a hand. As she went along, she became so wrapped up in her interpretation that she didn't stop to think about what she was saying. She cheerfully told the assembled company that it looked as if the man was having an affair outside his marriage. The gasp of surprise and the man's chalk-white face stopped her in her tracks. She then backtracked and suggested that perhaps the man had a hobby that took his time and attention. A few days later, someone in the know told her that his "hobby" was a fling with the woman who taught creative writing!

If the heart line is straight, the subject may find his work far more interesting than his companion. He may look down on his partner and consider her needs to be unimportant to him.

## Child Lines (Fig. 9.7)

These are fine vertical lines that are found near the edge of the hand on the mount of Mercury beneath the Mercury finger and usually crossing the attachment lines. These lines can be very deceptive and even experienced palmists find them difficult to read. The best way to read them is to hold the skin together between your thumb and forefinger. Roll the skin slightly, then try compressing and stretching the skin, looking at it through a magnifying glass. It is difficult to take clear prints of this area of the hand.

The theory is that each line represents a child but the lines can be confusing and the information less than absolutely reliable. However, if you want to try the method, this is how it should work. Child lines should be clear enough to stand out if they are to mean anything, and they should reach down through at least one of the attachment lines.

If you can see a line or lines, the person will probably become a natural parent and bring up a child or children. Sometimes a subject will actually have children but no corresponding lines or the lines may be so faint that they are easily missed in a poor light with the naked eye. In this case, the person may have children but he (or she) may not spend much time or energy in looking after them.

People who work with children or who look after them for others have a lot of these fine lines, but on close examination with a magnifying glass, they can be seen to approach, but not touch, the attachment lines.

## Sons or Daughters (Fig. 9.8)

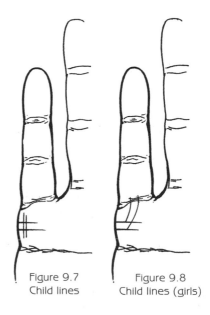

Some palmists hold the view that vertical lines indicate sons and lines that lean slightly toward the diagonal indicate daughters and this does seem to be true in many cases.

Figure 9.7
Child lines

Figure 9.8
Child lines (girls)

## Child Lines That Turn Away from the Attachment Lines (Fig. 9.9)

There may be friction that makes the child turn away from its parents. If, in addition, the subject's life line hugs the mount of Venus rather closely and the mount of Luna is insignificant, the subject's placid, homely attitude could frustrate a child who wants to branch out and broaden his horizons.

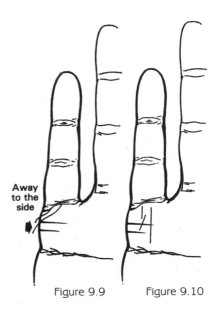

## Broken Child Line (Fig. 9.10)

There may be a difficult relationship between the child and the subject or possibly something physically wrong with the child. Either way it signifies that the relationship is not easy. An island on a child line shows temporary health or other worries.

Away to the side

Figure 9.9          Figure 9.10

## The Girdle of Venus

This line is a kind of supplement to the heart line and it is a sign of sensitivity. Sometimes the girdle is complete but in most cases, only part of it exists. The girdle is found on elegant or rounded type hands, long fine hands and even rather bony hands. It is least likely to be seen on broad square-shaped hands, thick fleshy ones, spatulate hands or extremely long and narrow hands with grasping fingers and curled nails. With luck, the presence of all or part of the girdle endows artistic or creative gifts. It is a good mark to find on the hand of someone employed in one of the caring professions because it shows that the person can understand the pain of others. This subject is easily moved to tears by a sad film or beautiful music. Even if the person exhibits an *apparently* hard exterior he will be nursing a very soft center and longs for love and understanding.

A writer with this mark can express himself in poetic and romantic terms. An artist or musician lacking this mark would turn out work that may be technically brilliant but emotionally sterile.

## The Bad News

It is true that the girdle of Venus has a very bad press in most palmistry books because it is said to show that the subject is hysterical and over-emotional. This person has little self-esteem and he is extremely vulnerable. When others bully or harass him, he blames himself rather than them—sometimes for not knowing how to protect himself against them. He internalizes his anger and he suffers deeply. He may release his feelings by self-destructive habits or behavior. The subject may overreact to imagined slights, and he will never forget or forgive an insult or those who seek to hurt him. Once he loses trust, he may appear to go on as normal, but he will never really love or trust that person again. This subject is idealistic, unrealistic and apt to become disenchanted when life fails to come up to his expectations. Coupled with a straight heart line, this can lead to loneliness and emotional withdrawal.

We have noticed that this type of line harks back to a childhood where the person was criticized too harshly, compared unfavorably with others or in some other way damaged. He lacks a sense of self-worth and is always insecure.

## The Girdle of Venus with Many Attachment Lines

This shows difficulty in staying faithful to one partner, possibly because the subject is always searching for the perfect mate.

## Love and the Girdle of Venus

These over-romantic subjects will suffer badly from puppy love when young. Then, having learned the hard way just how painful love can be, will go head over heels another couple of times at least just to rub the message in.

## Fragments of the Girdle (Fig. 9.11)

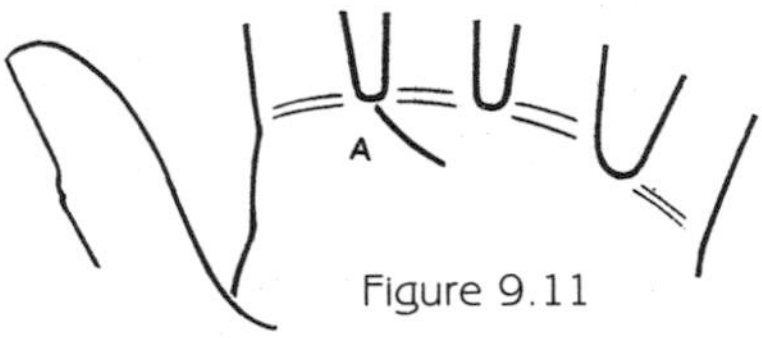

The area that a complete girdle would encompass can be divided into three sections: A, B and C. If only part of the girdle is visible, then refer to the relevant section.

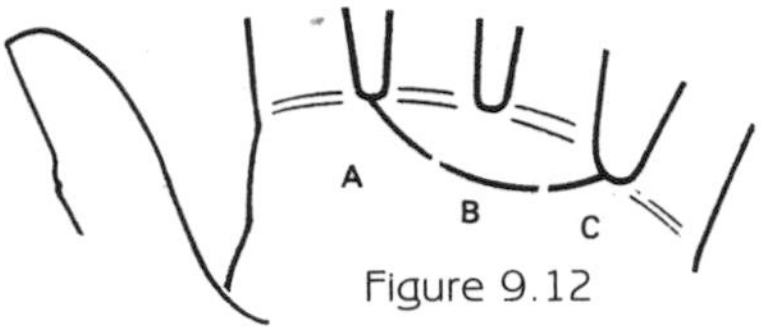

Figure 9.11

Figure 9.12

## Section of the Girdle of Venus (Fig. 9.12)

This starts under the Jupiter finger (A) or between the Jupiter and Saturn fingers. It curls around under the Saturn finger. Its presence shows the need for emotional security and for respect, career and financial security. If this section extends into section B the subject will be prepared to disrupt his personal life in order to achieve his career aims. If, in addition, the lower part of the life line extends outwards toward the fate line, this subject will sacrifice personal life in favor of a career.

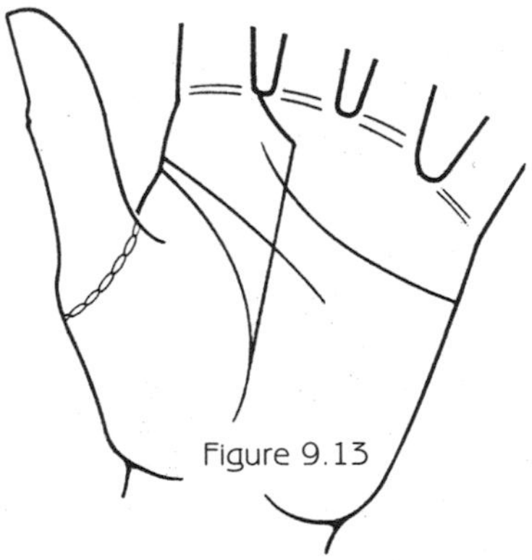

Figure 9.13

*(Fig. 9.13)*

When the fate line runs into section A of the girdle, and the life line reaches out toward the fate line, then the subject is definitely career-minded and he will put his heart and soul into his work. If the life line curves fairly tightly

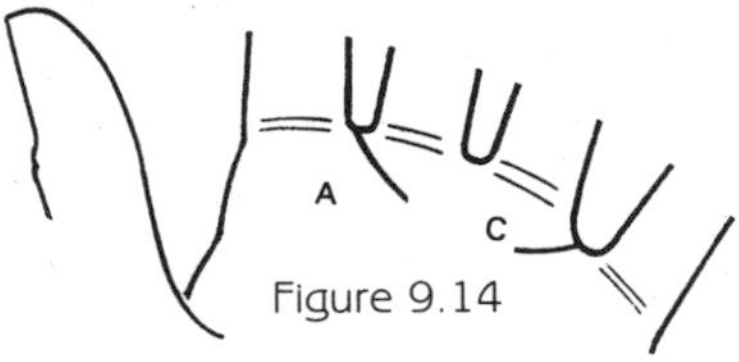

Figure 9.14

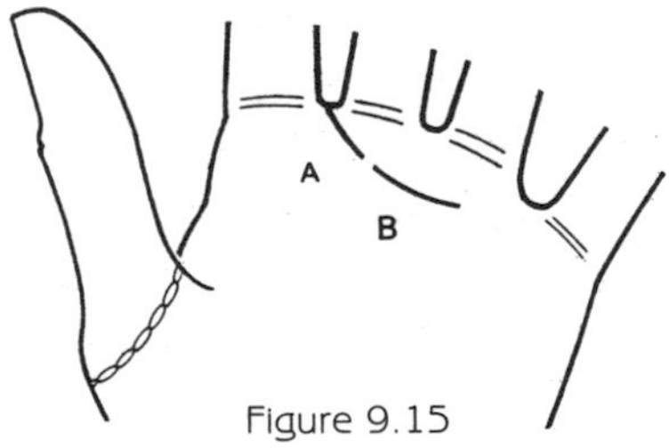

Figure 9.15

around the base of the mount of Venus, he will look for emotional fulfillment rather than a career.

*(Fig. 9.14)*
If the subject has section A and C of the girdle but not section B, he will relate to people on an intellectual level. He might become infatuated with a teacher at school, be taken in by someone with the gift of the gab, or be drawn to someone who understands him on a spiritual level.

*(Fig. 9.15)*
When sections A and B are present, the subject could walk out on a marriage if it interfered with his personal ambitions. He could react badly to the onset of middle age by throwing over a relationship and looking for excitement elsewhere or seeking out an unsuitable younger partner.

Section C lies between the Apollo and Mercury fingers and curls down under the Apollo fingers. This person wants to be around like-minded people and he needs them to understand him and to be on his emotional or spiritual wavelength. He may be intellectual and he is certainly choosy about who he associates with. He may choose people who can teach him something, as he is impressionable and wants to learn. If this subject married when young, he may discover later in life that he has little in common with his partner.

## Girdle of Venus Accompanied by a Tied Head and Life Line

This person was sensitive when young. He was shy, wary of other children and afraid of adults—probably with justification. If the head line curves down to Luna, the childish imagination adds to the situation and makes the child phobic—although he may have good reason to be fearful. Girdles heighten the effects of any trauma.

Traumas that occur at about the age of twenty to twenty-one can be spotted on the mount of Neptune. There may be a short life line or an island on the southern end of the life line or fate line. In addition to the girdle, there may be a wart on the mount of Luna or Venus.

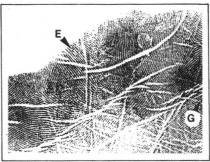

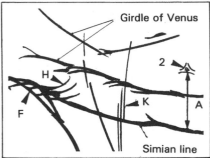

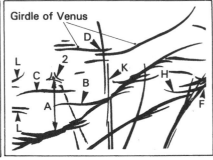

Figure 9.16a   Dominant right hand          Figure 9.16b   Minor left hand

## Case History: Robert (Fig. 9.16)

The print and illustration called Fig. 9.16a shows the dominant right hand, while the print and illustration called Fig. 9.16b shows the minor left hand. The prints from this young man show an unbroken girdle of Venus on the right hand and a very nearly continuous one on the left. Look at the girdle and the surrounding lines.

- These exceptionally strong girdles cloud Robert's thinking and affect his daily life. He happens to have a whorl on the finger of Apollo that tells us that he can only see his own point of view and that he is self-absorbed where matters of love are concerned.

- Notice the isolated line on the left hand that is near the lines of affection (c). Is this another girdle or a stunted attempt at an extra heart line? If so, this would indicate a lively and animated character. To find the answer to this we must look for a datum point on both of the hands. The datum points are the tri-radii that are marked 2, and which appear on both hands.

- Look at the left hand. Take a line (A) down the hand from the tri-radii. This is the same length as the line (A) on the left hand. This will cross the isolated line and land on a strangely thickened part of the heart line.
- On the right hand, a path drawn down from the tri-radii ends up on a peculiar addition to the head line which is in fact an embryo simian line. Robert knows deep down what love is but he is so mixed up that he is unable to express it!
- The strong attachment lines show that he is interested in marriage. He will change in his mid-thirties when the Apollo line crosses the girdle.
- The line girdle actually breaks (D) the strangle-hold of the girdle in the left hand as it crosses it.
- There is a strong line that flicks upwards from the heart line reaching up toward the attachment line (B), which shows him reaching out toward a relationship.
- He knows how to flirt because the fine lines that fall down from the heart line show this. Flirting keeps him in touch with the opposite sex, which gives him the chance to learn a little more about his feelings.
- The tri-radii on the mount of Mercury show his desire to communicate, and the girdle shows his need to be understood, but the heart line of affections shows self-consciousness. Difficult early experiences or even some doubt as to his sexual nature or the quality of his performance may haunt him while he is young.
- If the area between Mercury and Apollo is high, then he may find it easier to talk to animals (or computers) than humans, but he could make use of the loop of humor on his left hand (E) to cover up awkwardness and embarrassment. The humor loop curls under the finger of Apollo, and this denotes a sense of style and some vanity. Coupled with the whorl on the Apollo finger, this might indicate that he could fear a loss of composure during lovemaking or a loss of control over his life if he were to fall deeply in love.
- The cat's cradle effect (F) on the tied life and head lines and heavy crossing family lines (G) from the mount of Venus, suggest that he found his teenage years very difficult. He may have hated school or college or he may have bent over backwards to please hyper-critical parents. The upward flick on the head/life line (H)

shows that he could have dreamed about getting out of the situation. He seems to be a dutiful son.

- The change in the Apollo line suggests that his confidence grows later when he makes a success of himself at work. This would have to be backed up by nice clear successful-looking head and fate lines.
- The relationship that is due to happen in his thirties (K) suggests that he is definitely interested in marriage but finds it hard to be totally committed. He could become disappointed when he discovers that his woman turns out to be human and not the sugarplum fairy. This is shown by the doubled attachment lines (L).
- He needs freedom so that he can put his energy into other projects. He may also select partners who have problems because he is gifted with sympathy and understanding. The partner's problems and responsibilities sometimes show up as companion lines to the attachment lines (L). This subject is prepared to look after a lover, but may keep his real needs well hidden for fear of rejection.
- Robert's hand shows that he uses a variety of survival mechanisms to get through life. Good experiences will help to offset his super-sensitivity while unfortunate ones will reinforce his poor self-image and increase the risk of him destroying potentially good relationships.

## Case History: Peter (Fig. 9.17)

Here we see a man who is still living at home at a time when he should be out on his own, because he is caught between his own oversensitive nature and the demands of parents who do not want to relinquish their control over him.

- Peter has a weak-looking life line which suggests that he has a low level of physical energy, little zest for life and that he lacks self-confidence.
- The line of Mars (or companion line to the life line) shows that he can draw on extra strength when under severe pressure.
- He has a long sloping head line which shows a very active imagination, and a wart on the mount of Luna which suggests that he is fearful—although this condition is temporary rather than permanent.

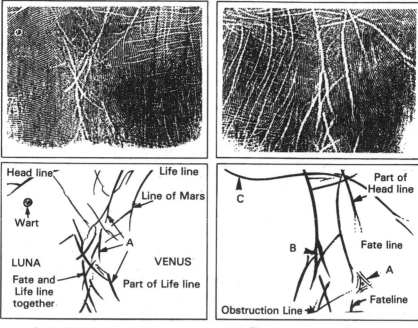

Figure 9.17   Minor left hand                    Figure 9.18   Dominant right hand

- The broken bits of life line (A) suggests that he wants to become independent and to have a home and family of his own, but the inner confusion, coupled with his overprotective parents, make it hard for him.
- If Peter screwed up his courage and broke out of his paralysis, the lines would start to grow a little clearer and the wart would drop off—which shows that he could change is fate if he tried.

## Case History: Kevin (Fig. 9.18)

This print was taken from a young man about five years *before* he was involved in a tragic accident.

- An obstruction line comes from the chained family line (C). The obstruction line crosses a busy junction of the fate and head lines and meets another stray obstruction line reaching out from the life line.

- The accident occurred when Kevin and his friend were out on their motorcycles on a country road. His friend's bike went out of control, hit an embankment and skidded across the road in front of him, giving him no time to get out of the way. He drove straight into his friend and killed him outright. There was no way that he could have avoided this.
- The junctions where the lines cross the steeply sloping head line show the disturbing effect on his mind. The tri-radii (A) that appear in the gap in the fate line, in addition to the island (B) on the life line show that he will have to find a way of coming to terms with the accident.
- There seems to be another lesser trauma on the way at the age of twenty-four. Perhaps this may give him an opportunity to bring this event out into the open and then put it away into the past perspective.

## Sibling Lines (Fig. 9.19)

Sibling lines are located on the edge of the hand on the *radial* side of the mount of Jupiter. They look rather like the attachment lines and their meaning is similar, but the relationships that they are concerned with are with brothers, sisters, cousins and those who feel like same-age relatives. Malcolm has always associated these lines with people who can adapt to a variety of jobs. These ideas might be connected, because someone who grew up in

Figure 9.19

a rough and tumble environment with other children around is more adaptable than someone who was a single child among adults.

It would be nice to say that one line equals one sibling, two equal two siblings and so on, but what seems to be shown is the way we feel about siblings, etc. If there is a relationship in the past or still ongoing, which may be loving or difficult, there will be a line or lines.

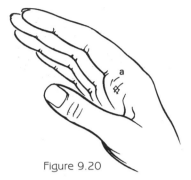

Figure 9.20

## Square, Cross, Star, Discoloration or Any Mark on a Sibling Line (Fig. 9.20b)

A square is a sign of protection or frustration. It suggests that a sibling is hemmed in by problems and that the subject is aware of this.

## Sasha's Tale (Fig. 9.21)

I became aware of these lines while giving a reading a few years ago. The lady whose hand I was reading had a great deal of redness and a strange starry formation on and around one of these lines. On impulse I asked her if she had a sister or brother who was having problems. She told me that her sister had just given birth to a first child and that it was a Down's syndrome baby. She said that her sister was utterly pole-axed

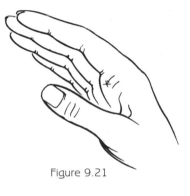

Figure 9.21

by this, and that although the sister's husband was a very kind and supportive man, he also seemed temporarily unable to cope. My client said that she would help in any way she could, and would probably become very involved in the upbringing of the child.

She never married and was successfully running her own business from home. She was in a position to give this child love and financial support that it needed, so it seemed that this baby was destined to bring love and fulfillment rather than disappointment.

# CHAPTER TEN

# THE MINOR LINES

## Via lasciva (Fig. 10.1)

This used to be called the poison or allergy line. Both are correct as an allergy shows that one man's meat is another man's poison. It is found on the mount of Luna and it travels toward Venus. The shape and size varies from one hand to another, as does the meaning.

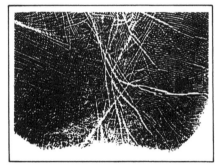

Figure 10.1

If the line stands out long and clear, the body and mind are sensitive to drugs, chemicals and certain foods. These people need only a small amount of any drug for the body to react so they tend to turn naturally to homeopathy and natural remedies. This line shows healing and self-healing abilities. Allergies are indicated when the line wraps around the percussion side of Luna, even if there is *no* via lasciva, but two or three strong lines on the percussion side of Luna indicate that the subject will still be sensitive to substances. If these lines show V formations at the side, there is even more evidence.

If the via lasciva is broken, islanded or surrounded by fine lines, the person may crave something. Food cravings, especially chocolate, are amazingly common when this line appears. It is also worth noting that this area of the hand is where we find evidence of diabetes. When the via lasciva reaches the life line, its effect will be more profound and there could even be slight brain damage due to anaesthetic at some stage! It is a good idea to look for islands, a "string of pearls" effect and damage to the head line for corroboration.

The via lasciva is confusing to interpret because it is on the area of the hand that is associated with travel. If it stands clean and clear on a hand that only has an average-sized mount of Luna and a life line that curls around the mount of Venus, the subject will not be especially interested in travel. If it is deep and seems to pull at the lower end of the life line, tugging it away from Venus, there could be at least one important journey overseas, probably in connection with family and friends who live abroad.

## Curve of Intuition (Fig. 10.2a)

This shows intuition and often also psychic gifts.

## Family Ring (Fig. 10.2b)

This shows the home base. If there are two rings the subject could be involved with two families or two homes. Dots and discoloration show problems while lines that radiate from here and cut across the

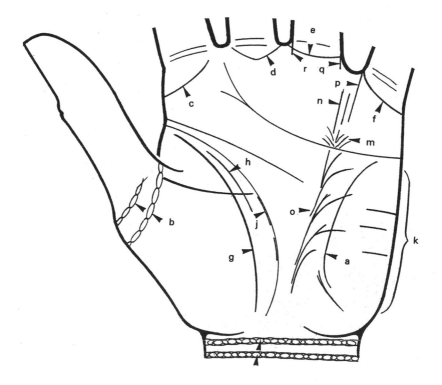

Figure 10.2   Minor lines

life line show interference from the family. A strong line like a light crease is frequently seen radiating out from the family line. If it reaches out and touches the life line, the subject feels a sense of loyalty to his family. If the crease turns northward, the subject loves his parents and looks back to the past. If it turns southward, he loves his partner and children and he looks to the future.

## Ring of Solomon (Fig. 10.2c)

Our friend, Sheila McGuirk, calls this the *caring line* because it can be seen on the hands of those who help others. If the heart line leads into the ring, the subject will only be happy working in a caring job and he may do so in place of normal family life.

## Ring of Saturn (Fig. 10.2d)

This is an unfortunate sign as it suppresses the personality and cuts off the balancing influence of the Saturn finger from the rest of the hand. This belongs to a lone wolf who finds it difficult to relate to others and join in with social activities.

## Ring of Apollo (Fig. 10.2e)

There is no specific meaning to this mark other than some kind of blocking mechanism.

## Spinster Line (Fig. 10.2f)

This is sometimes called the ring of Mercury. This must be unbroken. It belongs to those who never settle down with a partner or who repeatedly lose partners—possibly through death.

## Line of Mars (Figs. 10.2g and 10.3)

This is sometimes called the sister line or inner life line because it sits on the inside of the life line. It is a strong line, which is often as deeply engraved as the life line itself. There are several interpretations for this, the usual one being that it provides strength and protection to the part of the life line that it follows. This is especially so if the life line is chained, broken or islanded. We have found that people with this line overcome illness or accidents and they seem to be less open to viruses than others. If this line travels for the length of the life line (as the print shows), the protection will last throughout life.

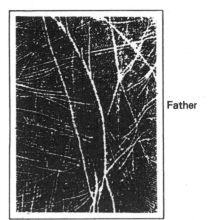

Father

The line can enter the hand at any age and stay to help during certain phases of life. The Mars line can relate to an inner spiritual pathway, giving protection and awareness of the spiritual self. The line may come and go in the hand as the spiritual interplay goes on.

The line of Mars is found on the hands of healers and others with an inner calling. The prints *(Fig. 10.3)* which we have shown are of a father and daughter. The father is a medium and healer but the daughter is too young to have discovered any particular spiritual pathway yet. The father says that he has always felt inwardly guided.

Daughter

Figure 10.3

## Medial Line (Fig. 10.2h)

This lies between the line of Mars and the life line and indicates that there was some sort of an early start that was quickly recognized as being wrong. The subject may have married in order to please the parents, gone to university or gone into a career that was designed to live out the parents' dreams. The difference between this and the line of Mars is that the person is more likely to put up with the problem and live through it rather than to go his own way.

## Shadow Lines (Fig. 10.2j)

You will sometimes see a fine tracery of two or three lines accompanying the life line around Venus. These are said to show friendships, but they also seem to show spirit guides or dead members of the subject's family still keeping a fond and helpful eye on him.

A variety of lines on the mount of Venus can show material success and an attachment to the home, possessions, furniture, car, jewelry, ornaments and things in general. These sometimes also denote affectionate friendships.

## Travel Lines (Fig. 10.2k)

These are on the percussion and may or may not include the via lasciva among them. They can appear at any point from the heart line down to the wrist. Many faint marks around the percussion are a sign of restlessness but not necessarily real journeys. One or two deep lines will show few trips, but these may be long-distance and they are certainly memorable.

If one or two of the lines join up with the fate, Apollo or any other northward travelling line, the journeys will have a purpose, so they could be in connection with business or with family who live overseas. Other indications of travel are a life line that reaches outward toward Luna, a high mount of Luna or a mount of Pluto (lower Luna) that reaches down toward the rascettes.

## Health Line (Fig. 10.2o)

This is a very confusing line. It appears on the hands of the healthy as well as those who are sick and is often seen on the hands of healers, nurses and other people who look after the sick. It shows up strongly on the hands of people who look after sick relatives or bring up delicate children. The healing lines *(Fig. 10.2n)* are an extension of the health line. Time and time again we have noticed that people who quite unwittingly have healing abilities are drawn to those who need help and it is as though a hidden force gives these people a spiritual push. If you take a look at the hands of a healer after he has used his gifts, you will see a reddish patch under the health line, and this will fade away after an hour or so.

If the line is broken up and flakes upward and outward toward the ulna side as illustrated, there could be heavy responsibilities on behalf of sick relatives. Check for lines that radiate out from Venus. This formation is also found on the hands of people who try to control their children by giving or sacrificing to them as a form of keeping them dependent.

## Healing Striate (Fig. 10.2n)

There can be two, three or more lines and sometimes a diagonal line crosses them. Not only doctors and nurses have this, but also spiritual healers, counselors, psychiatrists, hypnotherapists and any other person who helps in a specialized way. These people are very good at helping their family and friends, and do so without complaining. They appear to be spiritually directed toward helping and caring.

## Helping Lines (Fig. 10.2m)

These are lots of fine lines rising from the heart line as illustrated, and belong to people who work for or with the general public.

## Line Leading to the Inside of the Mercury Finger (Fig. 10.2p)

This symbolizes a gift for teaching. The teaching will be more formal if there is another line converging, and more spiritual and mediumistic if the line is connected to the healing striate.

## Fine Lines between Mercury and Apollo (Fig. 10.2q)

This shows spiritual growth and consciousness gained by the spiritual self on this earth. If light shows through when the fingers are closed, the subconscious mind is open to unknown forces. These lines may connect with the c section of the girdle of Venus, which suggests a need to be with people who share the same interests.

## Fine Lines on the Inside of Apollo on the Saturn Side (Fig. 10.2r)

Two parallel lines show that the person will never be alone in life. If these lines converge, the subject will never be without a physical and emotional relationship. These connection lines appear at the end of a lifespan, so the subject can expect to meet his friends and relatives in his next incarnation.

## Trident on the Mount of Apollo

Three little lines like the forks of a trident at the top of the Apollo mount show that the subject will always find money from some-where. Even when debts begin to pile up, these people will be able to find money in the nick of time. A blank area at the top of Apollo means financial losses or that something is wrong with the home.

## Travel and Countries (Fig. 10.4)

These lines show where a person goes on his travels. There is no logic to this, but it works. Just see where the lines are and check with your subject for confirmation. Place the percussion side of your own hand onto the picture lining up your heart line with the heart line in the picture. Then look at the countries you are likely to visit:

(a) Between the heart and head line: Scandinavia and Europe.
(b) Around the end of the head line: Eastern Europe, the eastern Mediterranean and the Middle East. Oddly enough, important business dealings rather than actual travel can also turn up here.
(c) Long strong lines on the Mars/Luna junction: the United States, Canada, the Caribbean and South America.
(d) Mid Luna: India, Sri Lanka and Seychelles.
(e) Lower Luna: China, Korea and Japan.
(f) Pluto: Australia and New Zealand.

## Travel Lines That Tug at the Life Line (Fig. 10.5)

Sometimes a travel line touches a branch which shoots out from the life line and this relates to some long-term involvement with a

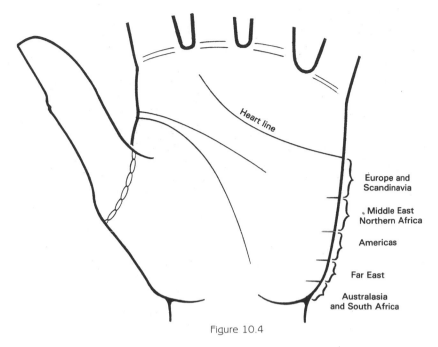

Figure 10.4

foreign country. This obviously creates an interest in the politics and economics of that country which would not have arisen otherwise. Of course there would be visits to the country in question and possibly a genuine link developing with its people and culture.

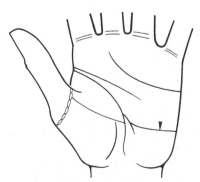

Figure 10.5 This kind of formation would be found on the hands of someone who had links with Canada or the United States.

## Example: Sarah (Fig. 10.6)

Sarah was born in the United States and came to England at the age of twenty-three and has stayed here ever since. The line coming from the point where the family line touches the life line relates to the way that another country tugged at her life line.

Figure 10.6                                          Figure 10.7

## Example: Jennifer (Fig. 10.7)

Jennifer is now twenty-two and she is working in England for the time being. She knows that when her work permit runs out she will have to return to Pakistan. Apart from the travel line touching the life line there is a hint of her apprehension in the line from Venus that is just under the skin.

## Example: Lawrence (Fig. 10.8)

Lawrence is seven years old. He was born in Switzerland, but his family took him to live in Argentina. It is interesting to note that in his mother's hand there is a line running from the family line to the correct position for Argentina.

Figure 10.8

## Change of Location: Rita (Fig. 10.9)

This broken-up life line looks as if it belongs to a person whose life is filled with drama, but it belongs to someone who has already made her home in a country other than her own and seems to be about to do the same thing again.

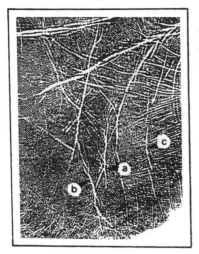

Figure 10.9

Rita was born to a lower middle-class family in Ireland forty years ago. She came to London to train as a nurse (a and b), then she married an Englishman and began to make her home in London. The marriage did not last very long so Rita divorced and married another Englishman some time later. This marriage was not too successful either but it was bearable. Also they had children. Now she and her husband are about to move to Hong Kong due to his job. Rita is looking forward to her new life in Hong Kong, but feels that she will come back to London eventually. She still keeps in touch with the remnants of her family in Ireland (c) but feels less and less Irish as her life goes on. She says that she can see herself losing all the links with her birthplace as the years progress. The faint line of Mars (c) shows that there are still some ties of blood or sentiment to the land of her birth.

## Military Marks (Fig. 10.10)

These marks are traditionally supposed to belong to people who spend their lives in the armed services, but it also appears when the subject comes from a military family. This can also turn up when the person is in the scout or cadet movement or something similar or a woman who is a service wife.

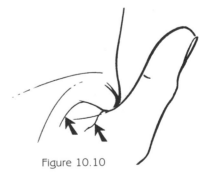

Figure 10.10

# CHAPTER ELEVEN

# MARKS

The meaning of each mark varies according to the line or mount on which it appears. Each mark should be clear and if possible, backed up by supporting evidence elsewhere on the hand. Marks are often *temporary* features that appear before an event and fade away some time after.

## Crosses on Lines (Figs. 11.1 and 11.2)

Figure 11.1

A cross on the life line can indicate a shock, an emotional upheaval or an illness. Check the finger nails for horizontal ridges, which would confirm a shock to the system during previous months. If on the fate line, there is some kind of setback or upheaval.

A series of crosses down the Apollo or health lines often mean that the person works

Figure 11.2

in or is associated with a large building that has many rooms. A cross on Apollo can sometimes indicate that the person is buying or selling property at the time of the reading.

## Crosses on Mounts (Figs. 11.1 and 11.2)

A cross on Apollo signifies a win, bonus or a nice surprise. This may be a lucky business deal or money that simply came along. A cross on the mount of Jupiter can mean marriage to a wealthy partner or an interest in teaching. When on the mount of Mercury, the person will be involved with appliances, machinery or office machinery.

The so-called mystic cross that is supposed to be between the heart and head lines is usually made from bits of the fate line and an influence line. Neither of us thinks this is a reliable indication of psychic powers.

Crosses on the side of the first phalange of the Saturn finger symbolize living near large animals, especially horses. In addition, a child line going into the crease line on the Mercury finger may mean working with animals.

Sheila McGuirk tells us that a cross on Luna means that the subject is prone to seasickness and possibly to other forms of travel sickness as well. She discovered this because she herself is not a good sailor and has checked this with other travelers.

## Squares (Fig. 11.3)

A square is like a fence around a building. It protects it but it also restricts free passage, so a square can indicate a miraculous escape from danger or, on the other hand, sadness and frustration.

Figure 11.3

A square on the life line shows recovery from danger and sickness. When on the head line it can protect the head and upper body from danger. An elderly client of ours told us that many years before, she had fallen from a horse while hunting and had narrowly missed having her head stamped on by one of the following horses.

A cross on any line symbolizes protection when it is deeply etched. If it is fine, it may be a transitory sign of frustration, restriction or sadness. These light covering marks come and go fairly easily and if the person changes his situation the mark will fade.

## Case History: Pat (Fig. 11.4)

The print shows a split on the fate line (a) covered by a square (b) that coincides with a time when Pat's life was exceptionally difficult. Her husband had left her with no money and four small children—one of whom was mentally handicapped. She used her considerable courage and reserves, as shown by the effort line (c) rising from the life line (d), plus the decision lines (e) that forced her to accept change (f). Pat found a job in the accounts section of a local firm (g) that gave her the money to cope. Success and job satisfaction then compensated for the hardship of her personal life. She also made some good women friends at that time which gave her practical and moral support (h). Later on, Pat met another man and had a happy and settled second marriage, but this whole experience left her with a fear of poverty.

## Squares on Mounts

This usually means protection or restriction in the area of life described by the mount in question. A square on Jupiter protects against loss in business. It can also indicate idealism or teaching gifts. Incidentally, small lines that rise up from the life line to this mount also indicate idealism.

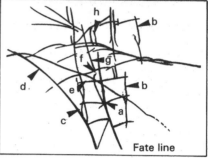

Figure 11.4

## Triangles and Diamonds (Fig. 11.5)

A triangle on the head line signifies intense frustration and feelings of confinement. This could result from a long spell in hospital, prison or simply exceptionally frustrating and confining circumstances at the time that is shown.

Isolated triangles on mounts are a sign of exceptional talent, even brilliance. The mount will indicate the relevant field. A large triangle between the head and heart lines is traditionally supposed, like the mystic cross, to signify strong psychic powers. We have no evidence of this.

Figure 11.5

## Stars (Fig. 11.6)

A star is traditionally a malevolent sign. It inten-
sifies energies at its location and acts like a stone
that pierces and cracks a pane of glass. It could
indicate a shock or an accident. A star on Apollo
is traditionally supposed to indicate fame and
fortune.

Figure 11.6

## Grilles (Fig. 11.7)

Figure 11.7

Densely packed lines mean an overabundance of
energy—perhaps even hyperactivity. Vertical lines
mean excessive desires while horizontal lines can
denote cross purposes or confusion. Therefore, a
grille points to obsessive behavior that takes its
nature from the mount it appears on. If on Venus, it
concerns an obsessive desire for something or some-
one, while on Jupiter it may relate to an obsessive need to be boss.

Grilles also mean severe illness or a shock to the system such as an
injury or operation. Once the body recovers, the grille goes.

Small vertical lines or grille formations around lower Mars show
an ability to keep secrets. A clean area shows that the subject has no
interest in secrecy for himself and he may not see why other people
want to be secretive.

## Tassels (Fig. 11.8)

Two or more lines flaking away from the main line and running close
to each other indicate a loss of
energy from that line. In our
example on the head line, there
may be a lack of calcium fluoride
or potassium or a great deal of
worry. This may signify depression or even senile dementia. Tassels
on the heart line are completely different.

Figure 11.8

## Dots (Fig. 11.9)

Dots are always important. They show illness and stress at the time of the reading.
They are miniature craters that suck energy downwards away from the line or
mount on which they appear. The body
may be using more energy than it is producing and the subject will soon outrun

Figure 11.9

his natural reserves. Dots of stress can be vitally important if seen
on the health area of the heart line. A dot on the head line shows
anxiety; other dots have to be read according to the line they are on.

Sasha's first husband was once rushed to the hospital with a kidney stone. Palmists are dreadfully ghoulish, so while he was waiting
in the emergency room and in dreadful pain, Sasha checked out his
hand. Sure enough, there was a clear crater on his health line. This
disappeared once the stone had broken up and passed through his
system and the kidney had recovered.

Use a magnifying glass to see these small marks. When a dot or
crater has a ring around it, this shows that the original cause of the
illness or upset is leaving the subject. A good example of this can be
seen on the health area of the heart lines of people who are getting
over heart troubles.

## Chains (Fig. 11.10)

A subject with chained lines lacks
stamina, assertiveness and confi-
dence. He may have weak health or

Figure 11.10

just a rather lifeless and ineffective
character. If only part of a line is chained, the person will go through
a difficult confusing time or a period of weak health. The line that is
affected and the placement of the chaining will indicate the nature
and the date of the difficulty.

## Islands (Fig. 11.11)

These must be taken into account in any read-
ing. An island represents a problem, which
might be health, troubles in relationships,

Figure 11.11

money worries, work problems or any one of a hundred things. The important thing to remember is that an island is an event that is difficult to live through because it splits the energies of the line it appears upon.

Always check whether an island is an isolated configuration, which is probably a health matter, or if there are disturbances on other lines, as this would lead one to suspect the onset of a sudden and life-changing event.

## Other signs

Blotchy or discolored patches, areas that appear shiny, faded or peculiar in some way usually indicate a health problem. Red areas show anger or tension, according to the line or mount.

## Branches on Lines (Fig. 11.12)

Branches that rise up from lines show improvements in situations, while falling branches show losses and setbacks. On the heart line, falling lines are traditionally supposed to be losses in love, but we have found short ones to be a sign of flirtatiousness.

Figure 11.12

## Islands Not Connected with Sickness (Fig. 11.13)

(a) A large island at the beginning of the life line denotes unhappiness in childhood.

(b) A thin island on the early part of the life line shows shock or upset. This is frequently the result of getting married early and facing up to adult reality!

(c) A long island or thin line close to the life line on the Venus side means a period of restriction. This could be due to caring for parents or children or studying. To some extent, the restriction is self-imposed.

(d) An island on the fate line shows a period of worry. This could be due to marriage problems, problems with children, financial difficulties or trouble at work.

(e) An island on a line, which leads into the fate line, suggests relationship difficulties.

## Influence Lines

(f) Fine lines running parallel to the life line on Venus show friendships and people who mean a lot to the subject. They may sometimes show an attachment to relatives or friends who are no longer living.

## Special Marks and Signs

(g) "Worry" lines that radiate out from Venus and cross other vertical lines are interference lines. If they cut through the life line or fate line, the subject will be forced to take some sort of action. If the lines peter out before reaching the life line, the problem is either hidden or becomes solved before coming out into the open.

## Decision Lines

(h) A fine line at an angle cutting the fate or Apollo lines from the radial side indicates that the subject will take the initiative over a decision.
(i) A fine line at an angle cutting the fate or Apollo lines from the ulna side indicates a decision made by someone else, possibly the spouse or partner, which will affect the subject. It may also indicate pressure being put on the subject so that he has to make a decision.
(j) A fine line cutting straight across the fate or Apollo lines is a blocking line that forces the subject to take action. This line can be very short or it may be traced back to Venus.
(k) A line joining the heart and head lines indicates a lack of communication in relationships. The marriage may even come to an end without the two parties talking things over and either or both partners will refuse to discuss anything. (This line must cut the fate line).

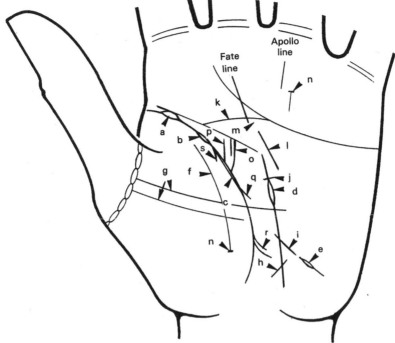

Figure 11.13   Special signs and marks in the hand

## Breaks and Interference on the Fate Line and Other Lines

(l) If there is a break but the lines overlap, the change will go smoothly. If the new line jumps toward the ulna side, there may be a setback or backward step, such as less money or not such a good job. If the fate line later moves toward Jupiter, the change will work out for the best.

(m) A gap in the fate line means a period of time out of work or a temporarily backward step in life.

(n) A small blocking line or dot at the end of a line may mean the death of someone close.

(o) Two lines, one going from the life line to the head line in the area illustrated, show restriction by parents. There may be a religious or arranged marriage. See also (c) in this section because both these marks are likely to show up in this case. The parents may be old-fashioned in their outlook or there may just be underlying pressure to marry someone who they deem to be suitable.

(p) Lines rising from the life line are effort lines. They show the times when the subject is trying to get over a bad patch or is setting out to achieve something for himself. If there is a dot at the base of the effort line, the subject may be getting over an operation.

(q) Small downward lines on the palm side of the life line could mean a change of home or job. Take a look at signs on the fate and Apollo lines to back this up.

(r) Longer lines indicate a restless period, a need for change or excitement in life. This is apparent when others try to interfere in the subject's life, especially if it cuts the fate line.

(s) Small downward lines from the life line on the Venus side *may* indicate the number of children but also losses of loved ones such as grandparents. These light lines tell of people who enter and leave the subject's life.

## Loops

Loop formation in the skin ridges on the palm are common, and while whorls are less common they have the same meaning as the loops but they are more intense.

## The Rajah Loop (Fig. 11.14a)

This unusual look, which sometimes has an additional tri-radius, reaches down between the Jupiter and Saturn fingers. It is supposed to bring power and status. People who have this loop are usually good looking, successful and arrogant. This is said to indicate that the person has royal blood or that they are descended from a leader in their society. Sasha remembers giving a reading to two brothers who both had these loops on both their hands. She commented about the possibility of royal blood. They were amazed by this and went on to tell her that they belonged to the Braganza family, which was once the royal family of Portugal!

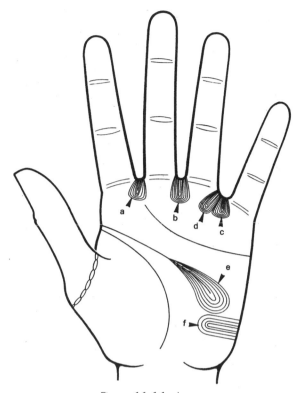

Figure 11.14   Loops

## The Loop of Serious Intent (Fig. 11.14b)

Located between the Saturn and Apollo fingers, this commonly seen loop indicates a serious turn of mind, someone who makes an effort to read, learn and understand and is also a hard worker.

## The Loop of Humor (Fig. 11.14c)

Located between Mercury and Apollo, this loop shows a sense of humor, also a love or words, writing, communicating and so on. If this area is high the person will also be fond of animals, but if the area is high and crossed by marks, the subject loves animals but has little time to devote to them. If the center of this loop forms a whorl, the subject has a talent for foreign languages.

## The Loop of Memory (Fig. 11.14e)

This loop is found near the end of the head line. It gives a good memory and also the ability to use contacts from one's past to help one in business. This person keeps in touch with people on a purely social level as well.

## The Loop of Imagination (Fig. 11.14f)

This loop indicates imagination and intuition that seems more likely to be used purposefully if near the Mars mount. A whorl shows psychic gifts. Loops in this Luna area also show a love of the countryside and of outdoor sports like fishing.

## Vanity Loop or Loop of Style (Fig. 11.14d)

Between Mercury and Apollo, reaching around beneath the Apollo finger, this loop is supposed to be a sign of vanity. We have found that people with this mark take pride in themselves and what they do and they have great personal style.

## Warts

If you want to get rid of a wart, cut a small piece of skin from a banana, place the inside of the skin over the wart and cover the whole thing with some plaster for a day or two. Keep doing this until the wart has gone.

According to the medical profession, a virus causes warts but in palmistry their cause is psychosomatic. They indicate long-term stress situations requiring changes that only we ourselves can bring about and problems that only we ourselves can overcome. The position of the wart gives a clue to its meaning.

- If found on the Jupiter mount or finger there would be something standing in the way of progress out in the world. Something affects subject's ambition and pride, causing a lack of confidence.
- Warts are most frequently found on the Saturn mount or finger, thus they relate to basic necessities, security, solvency and

survival. There may be career or money worries and the subject may be temporarily unable to provide himself and his family with a secure home.

- When on the Apollo mount or finger, a wart denotes difficulties connected to the home, children, relationships or perhaps a stifling of self-expression or creativity.
- On the Mercury mount or finger there could be communication problems—the subject could work or live alongside someone who deliberately misunderstands him.
- On the thumb the subject is unable to exert his will and he becomes frustrated.
- On the first phalange of any finger, there is mental anguish—on the other phalanges, there are practical problems.
- Warts on the hand should be read according to the line or mount. If, for example, there is a wart blocking the head line, the subject will not be thinking straight and may struggle at work or with studies.
- Warts on the back of the hand suggest problems caused by others, but those on the palm side signify that the subject himself needs to make changes in his lifestyle.
-  Warts that appear on children's hands are not important. They have more to do with the growing process and will go away again in time.

And finally . . .
Patches of redness on the back of the hands indicate problems caused by others. Read as per the finger or mount that patch refers to.

# CHAPTER TWELVE

# HEALTH

It is best to be a bit vague in this area of hand reading. If you really do think your subject has a problem, then suggest a visit to the doctor, but make it clear that you could be completely wrong even if you are certain you are right!

## Color

Hands should have a normal healthy color that is compatible with the race of the subject. The following information signifies health problems:

- Pale hands indicate poor circulation. Press the person's nail, and if it takes time for some color to return, they may be anemic.
- Blue or gray hands suggest artery problems.
- Yellow hands denote jaundice.
- Red hands could relate to hormonal problems, glandular trouble or high blood pressure. Smokers have red hands, but sometimes this just means that the person has a cold. Patches of redness may reflect emotional problems (check the line, mount and area of the hand).

## Temperature

- Hot, sweaty hands may denote a thyroid or other glandular disorder but some people are naturally hot.
- Hot, dry hands may indicate high blood pressure, kidney disorders or fever.
- Unnaturally cold hands indicate the onset of fever, poor circulation or they may be the result of a shock.
- Cold, clammy hands signify a sluggish liver.
- Cold patches denote uneven circulation and an uneven heart action, especially when the temperature varies around each finger.

- Run your finger up and down the end of the heart line at the ulna side. If the line seems to be hard and is in a dip, the blood pressure is high, but if the line is very soft, the pressure is low.

## Soft Hands

It is normal to have soft hands in old age; otherwise it is an indication of poor health, lack of energy and a nervous, fearful nature. When you see hands like these, look further for specific ailments. There may be a lack of protein through bad eating habits. The digestion system needs some kind of rhythm, so missed meals may account for this. Vegetarians usually have softer hands than meat-eaters and hands also become softer during pregnancy, so bear this in mind when looking at them.

## The Skin

Smooth, satiny, shiny skin suggests an overactive thyroid gland. Ask the subject to spread the hand out and then watch to see if there is a fine trembling. Rough, coarse, dry, cold hands with brittle nails suggest an underactive thyroid gland.

## Nails and Health (Fig. 12.1)

- Lateral ridges indicate a shock to the system that can be medical or emotional. A heavy indentation on all or most of the nails shows a heavy jolt that may be the result of an operation or even bereavement.
- Nails take around six to eight months to grow out depending on the state of health, so it is possible to date a

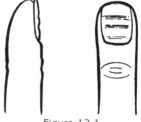

Figure 12.1

recent incident fairly accurately. Ridges that pile up one after another like waves running onto a sea shore show repeated shocks; therefore a period of sustained trauma. Ridges on the thumb show menstrual problems in a woman's hand. On either sex, these can show prolonged anxiety and frustration. This can also be due to palpitations or arrhythmia.

- Longitudinal Ridges *(Fig. 12.2)* show a number of complaints, but the most important is some problem relating to bones and their surroundings, such as cartilage, muscles, tendons and ligaments. There may be rheumatism, slipped discs, and old injuries that still leave a mark or strains and swellings of one kind or another. These are quite easy to map nail by nail. Another sign of rheumatism are bumps on the backs of the first phalanges or a thickened third phalange on the Jupiter fingers.

Figure 12.2

- Ridges on the thumb indicate problems with the back, neck and head, especially if these also appear on the Jupiter nail. The right thumb indicates problems on the right and the left thumb denotes problems on the left of the body. Lower back pain affects most of the thumb but leaves the center section a little clearer. Upper back pain affects the center of the nail. Thumbs are easily damaged, so don't go overboard with this.
- Ridges on Jupiter relate to the back and neck, while on Saturn they tell of pain in the rib cage, pelvis and hips. On Apollo, they reflect the arms, hands, legs and feet. On Mercury, they talk of the forearms, hands, lower legs, ankles and feet.

## Nails in General (Fig. 12.3)

- Tiny nails relate to the stomach, bladder and kidneys. If these nails seem to "sit" on the finger and the fingers are tapered or pointed, the subject is easily fatigued. He or she may have heart troubles, diabetes or may have some sort of glandular condition that leads to obesity.

Figure 12.3

- Watch-glass or "Hippocratic" nails have been known to medicine for centuries. The nails bulge upwards in the middle and turn under at the end. They show a shortage of oxygen in the blood due to lung or heart damage, and if the fingers are also clubbed at the end, the lungs are under severe pressure. This was traditionally a sign of tuberculosis but it can also indicate lung cancer or emphysema. If the lung/heart problem is temporary, the nails will grow back to normal once the trouble has gone, but if the lungs are scarred or the heart damaged, the end of the Jupiter and Saturn finger will always curl around the end of the finger. See Fig. 12.6 for asthma or lingering lung damage.

- Spoon-shaped nails *(Fig. 12.5)* denote nutritional deficiencies, an underactive thyroid or brain damage.

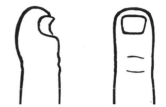

Figure 12.4

- White spots suggest some sort of vitamin or mineral deficiency. It could be shortage of calcium, magnesium or vitamin A or D. This is often due to a lack of sunshine, as these seem to show up on many hands in late spring. These can represent anxiety and depression.

Figure 12.5

- Dark patches under the nail that look similar to a dark bruise with a nail that is thick and ridged can be due to a fungal infection. Look at the toes for confirmation.

Figure 12.6          Figure 12.7

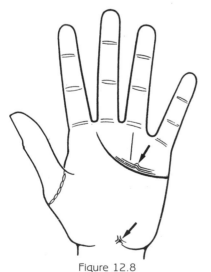

Figure 12.8

- Moons that are too large or missing can indicate heart problems but this is most likely to represent a problem if the moons change from what they were like before.
- When the end of the Mercury nail looks like a tunnel there is spinal trouble. *(Fig. 12.7)*
- An overgrowth of skin around the nails denotes psoriasis.
- Redness on the percussion mount shows glandular, especially thyroid, problems and it

may indicate blood-pressure trouble. This is often the sign of a smoker. Redness with fragmented lines, grilles and odd marks on Neptune shows problems in the uterus or possible pregnancy. On Luna and upper Mars, there may be diabetes or kidney disorders.

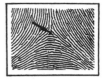

Figure 12.9

- A grille on Mercury indicates a sluggish liver. Grilles on the plain of Mars indicate liver and kidney problems and on Neptune, something wrong with the reproductive organs.
- The axial tri-radius *(Fig. 12.9)* of a healthy person is located directly above the wrist *(Fig 12.8)*. If it is misplaced it is symptomatic of heart disease.
- If the area around the heart line under Mercury and Apollo *(Fig. 12.8)* is hard to the touch, with lines running along the heart line which are "pushed" up by the hard lumpy area, there are heart problems.
- Dots, warts and even patches of eczema might point to problems in various parts of the body.

## Lines and Health

Dots and indentations on lines produce a "whirlpool" effect sucking energies down from the lines they appear on. Bars, crosses and breaks all indicate problems, setbacks or health problems. Islands often tell of health problems along with practical and emotional difficulties. Dots on the heart line near the percussion show the onset of a heart attack. If this area is messy or has large arrow-like fletches and islands, there could be a problem with the myocardium or the heart valves.

A heavily dotted life line shows spinal disorders. One or two dots might indicate a recent operation or other shock to the system. The main purpose of marks on the life line seems to be to date health problems rather than to identify them. Treat the life line as a spine with the top end (near the head line) as the neck area and the bottom end as the base. Very small islands show spine damage. A large egg-shaped island near Neptune concerns an impending disease that may turn out to be cancer.

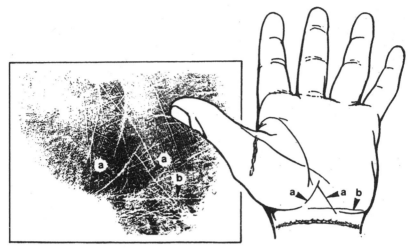

Figure 12.10

## The Rascettes (Fig. 12.10)

These lines run around the underside of the wrist like bracelets. They are traditionally supposed to indicate the length of life, each rascette being supposed to represent thirty years; therefore, three nice clear rascettes are said to equal ninety years of life. It is true that strong rascettes do show generally good health but it is the topmost rascette the one which is actually on the palm of the hand which is the most important. If this rascette is straight and clear, that is fine. If it loops upward into the hand there could be problems related to the reproductive organs. If the loop is full of strange little marks, there could be menstrual troubles or the subject may have recently had a hysterectomy. If the area is bitty and reddish, she may be pregnant or have recently given birth. An upward loop can also indicate throat or lung problems.

## Example: (Fig. 12.10)

The topmost rascette (b) sometimes shows the condition of the womb. The marks come and go quite quickly as the situation changes. The characteristic tent-shaped formation shown in the print (a) means that there is, or has been, some problem. In this case, the lady had two children by caesarian section. This kind of formation can arrive during pregnancy and gradually disappear after the womb has settled down again. If there is a triangle formation full of scattered bits of lines and the area has a reddish tinge, the subject may be in the early stages of pregnancy or possibly getting over a sterilization operation or some other disturbance of the reproductive area.

## The Head Line

- Breaks suggest accidents and injuries to the head. If these are not too serious, or were averted in some way, there will be a clearly marked square of protection around the break.
- Chains beneath the Saturn mount indicate headaches and migraine. Chaining can also be caused by the "rat in the trap" syndrome, where life is frustrating and unhappy. Islands here relate to eyes, and the subject usually wears (or needs) spectacles.

Figure 12.11

- Sugar tongs on the percussion side *(Fig. 12.11)* that enter the hand from the percussion and grab the end of the head line show insomnia. Insomniacs tend to have full hands.

## The Heart Line

The area of the heart line that lies under the Mercury finger is almost exclusively to do with health. About the only exception to this is the fact that chaining here could point to difficult relationships in youth. In this case, there will be evidence at the start of all the other lines.

- Islands close to the percussion edge denote lung trouble and dots on either side of the island show stress on the lungs. A "dent" in the line here indicates lung problems. Dots indicate a pending heart attack!
- Islands under Mercury show some strain associated with the throat and bronchial tubes (especially when found near the Apollo end). A dot at either end of the island or a dark color

is a sure indication of lung trouble. A long, rather lined, island here often indicates dental problems.

- If the heart line in this area shows a feathered effect, there will be some hardening of the arteries, possibly a tendency to develop angina.
- Islands under Saturn signify hearing problems.
- Dots warn of current acute health problems and inflammatory conditions.
- A star, circle, strange break, grille or other disturbance under Saturn where the heart line starts to curve upwards is a sure sign of breast problems. Sasha suffers from mastitis and has had operations for fibroids in this area and her hands carry grilles at this point.
- The health line does not seem to have much to do with health but it does show someone who is *interested* in health, either his own or that of others. A person who makes a point of eating the right things, taking exercise and living a good clean life in order to maintain good health will have a health line. There is some information to be gained about childbirth on the health line, especially down at the Luna end, but this fades some few years after the event.
- Tassels on the head and life lines show illnesses during the later stages of life. On the head line, this may be the onset of senility.
- Faded or blank patches indicate illness or emotional shock. Some years ago, a young client of ours looked after her younger brother and nursed her dying mother. Towards the latter stages of her mother's life, the grandmother came to stay and help. The grandmother was a kindly person but her ideas were totally different from those of the mother and the girl herself. The young girl developed a dramatic gap in her life line at that time, but when seen later, the break was gone. Our late friend John Lindsay commented when he heard this story that a gap in the life line does seem to show that the subject feels, at some point in his life, like a square peg in a round hole.

## String of Pearls

This nasty peculiarity arises when the skin ridges become broken up and badly formed. This can be due to emotional or psychological conflicts. When seen in children it is not terribly important because it is part of growing up, although it does point to emotional insecurity. In adults, it shows that the subject is living on his nerves. This may be caused by pushing the body beyond its limits at work or through a drinking problem.

## Case History: Henry, an Alcoholic (Fig. 12.12)

- Henry is now forty-nine years of age. He has been married twice, the second time at the age of thirty-five (a). He has had a history of psychological and drinking problems. The "string of pearls" is indicative of this type of problem, which is acidosis due to alcohol.

- Henry's short Jupiter finger (b) shows feelings of insecurity and inferiority and the curve toward Saturn shows emotional and sexual secretiveness. He finds it difficult to unwind and to be himself.

- There is an exceptionally flattened arch pattern (b) on three fingers and all three have many repression ridges beneath the arches. The fingers feel extremely rigid, showing a low tolerance to stress. There is also a weak thumb.

- Henry has coarse skin and soft hands that show that he is unwilling to listen to the advice of others and that he lacks protein.

- His watch-glass nails show heart and lung disease and in this case, cirrhosis of the liver.

- His broken life line (c) will not be able to supply enough energy to the head line. He does not know when to stop driving himself to the limit.

- The fate line near the life line in his case is indicative of alcoholism and dependency on others.

- A line (d) can be traced from lower Mars (childhood) cutting the fate line (lack of communication) then about to cut the Apollo line which ends in a wart (e). The wart shows us that only the subject himself has the answer to his problems.

- Both the Apollo and the fate lines fade out before their route is completed on the mounts at the northern end of the hand. The broken life line shows that when he reaches fifty-two years all his energies will be very low and he will be ill. The string of pearls substantiates this. There is too much stress on the nervous system and organs of the body.

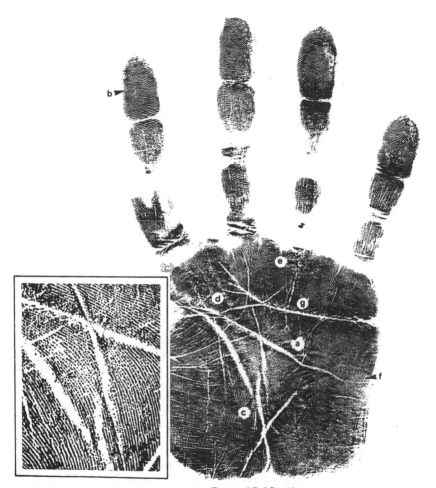

Figure 12.12   Henry

- The grille (f) on the ulna side by the head line shows toxic waste affecting the brain.
- Henry is at the end of his tether because his addiction has caught up with him. His wife left him two years previously (g) and now he has been turned out of the care hostel because of his drinking.

## Case History: Josie (Fig. 12.13)

This print was taken over a rolling pin in order to get a clear center section as the plain of Mars kept disappearing when we pressed Josie's hand directly onto the paper. The fact that her hand is hollow shows that she is a giver who sacrifices her life for her family's needs. Josie is forty-two years of age and she has a weak heart.

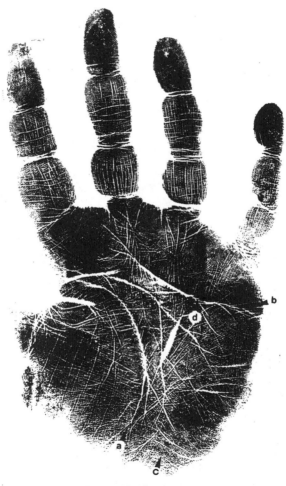

Figure 12.13   Josie

- All the major lines on Josie's hand, especially the life line (a), become tasseled and weak at the ends signifying a kind of giving up on life.
- The heart line under Mercury (b) is far too feathered for a woman of her age and the rascettes are breaking up (d). However the fate and Apollo lines reach the top of the palm which indicates a normal life span. The rather messy area at the bottom of the hand (c) suggests that her menstruation is giving her a problem. Although the confusion on this area of the hand may have arisen from a conflict between what other people tell her she should believe in and what she feels inside. The presence of the health line and healing striate show that she can recover, even from severe illness.
- There is a small sharply shaped island on the heart line under the Mercury/Apollo junction (which the print does not show clearly). Its presence shows that there has been a severe emotional shock some time in the past. This occurred a few years ago when her husband suddenly announced that he was leaving her for another woman.
- Josie had had a bad time giving birth to her only child, and this probably weakened her constitution. She also had rheumatic fever in her childhood. If that were the case, the myocardium (the skin around the heart, enclosing the coronary arteries) would have been damaged. The trauma caused by her husband's behavior brought on angina.
- It is interesting to note that there are an excessive number of lines showing up around the heart line in the area which indicates Josie's late thirties. This is typical evidence of an energy rhythm. There was more nervous energy stored up in her body than she could cope with at that time. This buildup of emotional and physical energy could have been released through work or exercise but Josie's rheumatism prevented her from exercising and she gave up work at that time due to nerves.

## Diabetes and Earth Death (Fig. 12.14)

The clue to diabetes is a pattern of fine lines coming away at an angle from the fate line and reappearing on Pluto. These fine lines are sometimes called a grille and may form a cross somewhere in that area. The print is that of a woman with a short life line. This woman died in her late fifties at the age where the life line terminates. If she had lived past that point, the life line would move over to touch the fate line and because the fate line is very fretted here, she would have been incapacitated. As it was, she was able to tend to the needs of her family until the very last.

Figure 12.14

## An Indication of Cancer (Fig. 12.15)

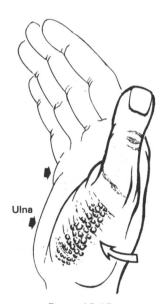

Ulna

Figure 12.15

If there is a cluster of small globules that have a transparent sheen that is either yellow or flesh colored, on the edge of the hand (on the radial side of the mount of Venus) this can be a sign of cancer. However, one must look for other signs, such as blue islands on the heart line and a large egg-shaped island on Neptune to substantiate this claim.

About a dozen years ago, Sasha was showing a friend of hers called Kay how to spot health problems on the hands and she mentioned these warty globules. Her friend pointed out that she had just those marks on her hands and that she had already had an operation for cancer of the cervix. Kay's cancer eventually came back and spread throughout her body. Tragically, Kay died at the age of 45.

## Health on the Child Lines

*(Fig 12.16a)*
A red dot or a pinprick hole shows miscarriage on the attachment line below the child line. A short stunted child line will sometimes show miscarriage or a stillborn child.

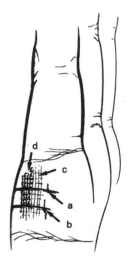

*(Fig. 12.16b)*
An abortion shows up in a similar way to a miscarriage. There will be a small crater on the attachment line beneath the child line with a small blue vein line coming from it.

*(Fig. 12.16c)*
A hysterectomy is shown by a lot of fine vertical lines covering the area of the attachment lines.

Figure 12.16

*(Fig. 12.16d)*
If the skin between the lines appears to glisten or take on a transparent sheen then the subject should be advised to take a smear test.

# CHAPTER THIRTEEN

# CASE HISTORIES

## Marie, an Actress (Fig. 13.1)

Marie has appeared on the stage and in television in many different roles. At the age of twenty-one she had pneumonia very badly and nearly died. Due to her own great efforts she recovered, although her lungs took a long time to restore themselves to normal health. At the age of twenty-nine she married. Her acting career prospered and her marriage faltered. By the age of thirty-eight she was divorced. She then married a man in the same profession as herself. This marriage too ran into difficulties, also, her career took a dive. She spent a good deal of time waiting at home for the telephone to ring with offers of work. Meanwhile she took a college course.

(a) Island on the heart line (lung trouble).
(b) Illness island.
(c) Life line almost parted.
(d) Double life line.
(e) Island with effort line.
(f) Strong new Apollo line going to the fate line.
(g) Fate line moves to radial side.
(i) Split in fate line with an influence line which can be traced from the family line to the attachment lines.
(h) Coming together.
(j) Common interests.
(k) Parallel line with a split (age fifty-three).
(f) Apollo line showing a return to home life.
(m) Hobbies and interests.

Figure 13.1  Marie

Figure 13.2   Chris

# Chris, an Ordinary Woman (Fig. 13.2)

The tracery of fine lines on Chris's hand shows that she is sensitive by nature and was feeling nervous at the time that the print was taken. Her long straight Jupiter finger that pulls away slightly from Saturn shows that she likes to think things out for herself. The head line that is lightly tied to the life line with a cat's cradle effect (a), plus the effort lines rising almost from the start of her life, tell us that she was not too happy as a child and she found it hard to concentrate while at school. Those early effort lines suggest idealism. The gap between the Saturn and Apollo fingers shows some inner rebelliousness. This kind of person always has difficulty during childhood because they do not conform—and childhood is all about behaving and conforming.

In the lower zone of the hand, the life and fate lines are separate but there is a heavy bar artificially tying them together (b). This bar seems to be imposed upon the other lines. This shows some confusion brought about by Chris's early need for freedom as against the restrictive nature of her upbringing. I would guess that there was a heavy religious influence in the parental home. This restriction and emphasis on correct behavior being imposed is reinforced by the line which trails down from the head line (c) showing that she married someone who her family considered suitable and the society in which she lived, rather than choosing someone for mental and physical attraction.

The clearly marked Apollo line which has its source at the life line (d) shows the desire for a stable and comfortable home. The peacock's eye on the Apollo finger gives taste and refinement, possibly artistic and musical appreciation as well. Her home must be an attractive place. The marks inside the Apollo finger (e) and the shadow lines that accompany the life line (f) tell us that Chris may be slightly mystical, even psychic. The loop of imagination and memory (g) on the Mars/Luna mount and the fairly full mount of Neptune give sensitivity and some understanding of people's unconscious motives; this is heightened by the fragmented girdle of Venus. This sensitivity and imaginativeness make her kind and understanding.

The head line bounces just on top of the large loop (g) endowing her with a good memory. She seems to be imaginative in her thinking rather than logical due to the northerly placement of the memory/imagination loop. The "waisted" second phalange of the thumb causes her to question things in order to find a logical explanation for the things that she can feel. The turned up end of the head line suggests business ability. The full mount of Mercury and slightly inward-turning Mercury finger denote shrewdness and acumen. Chris has no loop of serious intent (h), therefore she would find it hard to discipline her thoughts unless there was practical reason for doing so (hence the slim second phalange of the thumb).

The lines that enter the fate line at the age of twenty-two (i) show marriage after a long serious relationship. The long line entering the fate line and travelling to the life line shows that she could live close to her parents. The flick away from the fate line (j) a year or two later shows an ending and a decision. This decision to end something related to an affair which she had during the second year of marriage! At this point Chris matured enough to want to give up work and started a family. The doubling of the head and heart lines and life line from the age of around twenty-five to her late thirties shows confusion and split-mindedness about her duties toward her family. The line that travels toward and becomes parallel to the fate line (k) at about the age of thirty shows her going back to work again and splitting her energies between the family and her job. Note the presence of secretiveness marks on lower Mars and northern Venus (l). The long attachment line with the slight companion lines above and below (m) show that she solved the problems of being married to someone not entirely to her taste by having other interests. These interests may have included other liaisons. There is also a hint that she has been widowed in the past! This is shown by the bubble of shock (n) on the heart line and the influence line just where the heart line begins to split and bend (o). Chris's forked head line shows that she can be different people in different places, i.e. dedicated housewife, mother, business woman, worker, artist and entertainer (long Apollo finger with peacock-shaped whorl).

The segment of the girdle of Venus under the Apollo finger (p) plus the long head line and long first phalanges tell us that Chris is intelligent and likes to learn. She cultivates the company of those whom she considers to be older and wiser. Her loop of humor (q) shows her to be an attractive and spontaneous personality. The forked heart line shows that Chris wants to relate (r) to men but at the same time remain detached. She chooses her men for qualities which she finds socially rather than sexually attractive; she must be able to feel proud of them, because such a strong part of the heart line goes straight out to the lower part of the mount of Jupiter (s).

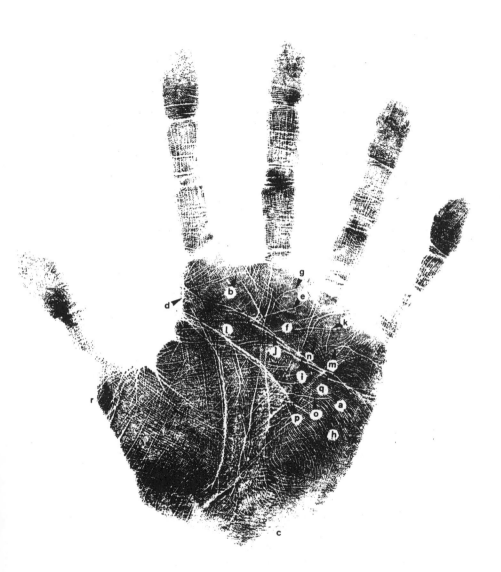

Figure 13.3

Although personally independent, Chris is both genuinely caring and also has a peculiar desire to control others by giving. This is shown by the flaky health line (a) which partly joins the attachment line. The flakes which run down from the heart line to the head line show some measure of uncertainty about her sexual nature. She could have some difficulty in relating to or trusting men. The upper part of the heart line (b) reaches into the ring of Solomon, which shows that Chris identifies herself as being a loveable person by helping, obliging and caring possibly in a slightly maternal way. She would probably prefer to make sure her man was well fed. Her caring identity is so strong that she probably does a lot for the young, old, sick or for animals. She needs a creative job with a caring outlet.

Chris's mind is restless and ambitious—this is shown by the slightly islanded, forked and flaky head line plus her ambitiously high mount of Jupiter with its tri-radius and the whorls on her fingertips. This battles slightly with her need for domestic harmony as shown by the life line which curves around Venus. Chris seems to have little desire to travel as the life line stays close to home, there are few travel lines and she has an inwards dent on the lower percussion at Pluto (c). The small sharply rising line on the edge of Jupiter (d) shows that she can make money for herself at a pinch.

There is an influence line crossing the fate line (e) at the age of forty-five and a bend in one of the Apollo line flakes which seems to show a new job very near the home. There is also a redefinition of relationships at this point shown by the breaks in the Apollo and fate lines (f). Chris seems to have come into money in her early fifties. This may have been as a result of a legacy, which is shown by the new addition to the fate line (g) that begins to travel to Apollo, plus the fact that the Apollo line seems to start on or inside the life line. This shows an increasing ability to obtain self-expression from life rather than just to live and earn money in order to put the family's food on the table. The upward flick at the end of the head line (h) shows her developing interest in business. There is some evidence of a death; this is shown by the shock island (i) on the heart line and the slight "snapping" of the heart (j) with an influence line just at that point. The evidence is corroborated by the position of the influence line (k) indicating the death of a relative or close friend. This could be how she has gained her freedom and found the money for a new start!

Chris's attitude is becoming gradually more adventurous now as shown by the outward flick at the bottom of the life line plus the rising optimism of the head and heart lines. She certainly has had some emotional issues to sort out. This is partly because of her caring attitude to love and also her preference for friendship rather than close sexual relationships. The majority of the heart line travels straight across to Jupiter with slight downward flicks (l). The long drooping attachment line shows a long-standing attachment to one man (m). This could be a boyfriend, but is just as likely to be the friendly suitable husband who stays nicely in the background while she explores her deeper feelings elsewhere! The drooping lines which fall from this attachment line (m) show that he frustrates her and leans upon her in some way, but her caring nature can cope with this.

One of these long drooping attachment lines shows that in her fifties she will have to look after elderly or sick relatives in or near the home. There are two branch lines going toward the home area (a) at the beginning of two vertical lines which suddenly end, thus showing the death of the elderly person.

There seem to have been business partnerships in the past as shown by the line entering the heart line (o). There will be others in the future as shown by the influence line entering and then crossing the head line (p). Chris's health is basically good although her lungs may be a little weak (q), therefore she should have plenty of life ahead of her to live and enjoy.

Just one final point. I am sure she likes dancing—but I don't know whether this has come to me by clairvoyance, or whether I am seeing it on the hand? Let us think for a moment. The long Apollo finger and Apollo line show artistry, the width across the Luna/Venus area shows an active person, the upward curve of the heart line shows sensuality (although in this case not sexuality), the angle of rhythm is strongly marked and the thumb is spoke-shaved which implies some desire to be popular. The restriction lines show that too much responsibility bores her and she needs to get away and have some fun on occasion. Active fun with her own sex, movement, music and a love of life seems to me to make her into a sportswoman or a good amateur dancer.

# Note

Malcolm had given me a print of Chris's hands to work from, but after writing most of this piece, he put me in touch with Chris, who confirmed my findings. There were a couple of minor adjustments to be made and some information to be added. Chris said that the most important factor in her life has been the restriction placed upon her by her demanding mother, who has lived with Chris on and off all her life. Mother is still alive at the age of ninety-two, still in good health and still getting her own way!

I was confused by the death and the legacy but Chris explained that a close friend had died and left her some money which she has indeed used in order to start a new and enjoyable business partnership. Chris also confirmed that she still *likes* her husband, she always did. She worries about him and wants him to be happy, but they no longer live together.

## The Anatomy of a Partnership: Malcolm (Fig. 13.4) and Sasha (Fig. 13.5)

Many people form partnerships for one purpose or another, but in the world of creative achievement, often nothing much comes of them. Why did this one work? What fate chose to bring us together and what special alchemy made the whole thing function so well?

We have supplied our own prints at this point so that you can work out for yourself why we both chose to make our living for so long by working as self-employed hand readers and why we found it so easy to collaborate on this project when, heaven knows, neither of us is easygoing. We have not given you any clues with this reading, no carefully placed letters to follow. We are leaving it to you to make your own assessments and to test your own hand-reading abilities.

Malcolm and I met in 1984 at the Festival of Mind, Body and Spirit at Olympia in London. We started chatting to each other about palmistry and found that we shared similar views. We both said how much we would like to write a book that swept away the ancient cobwebs and gave hand readers an original view.

I knew that I could write but I had no idea that Malcolm could illustrate. Malcolm did not know about word processing or realize that I had my own machine. It was only when we began serious discussions that it became clear that between us we had all the skills necessary for the job. As we got to know one another, we discovered that we have similar tastes and a firm friendship as well as a working partnership began to evolve.

Figure 13.4   Malcolm

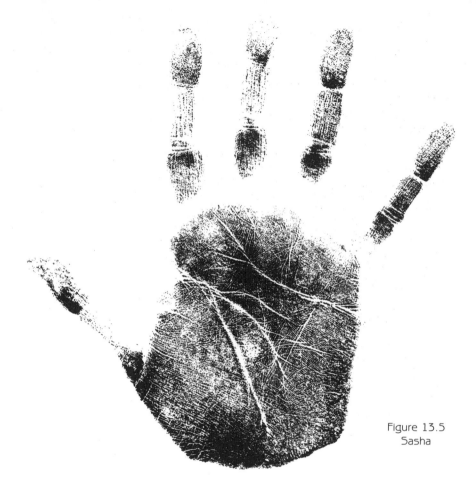

Figure 13.5
Sasha

## A Palmist's View of Sasha and Malcolm

### Similarities

Both hands are fairly long. Men's hands usually have fewer fine lines than women's but Malcolm's hands are fuller than usual for a man's while Sasha's are also pretty full. This shows that both of us are sensitive to hurt and able to link in with and understand the hurts of others. Neither hands have clear-cut main lines, all the lines are heavily branched, except for Sasha's heart line which is reasonably clear. This shows that we are both swept up by changing circumstances from time to time and both have many-faceted personalities. Both hands are long and square with a long palm. The mounts are rather flat. Both display life lines that reach outward, curved, sloping head lines with branches and curved heart lines with girdles of Venus. Both show confusion at the start of the head and life lines, indicating that our early lives were filled with difficulties. We share the same features of long strong thumbs, restriction and responsibility lines on the fingers and thumbs, family interference lines and only one strong attachment line. The need to please and to help other people is shown by loops of humor, rings of Solomon, health lines and healing striate.

### Differences

Malcolm is left-handed. Malcolm's hands are large with long fingers showing a love of detail, and the long third phalanges show that detailed work comes easily to him. Sasha's hand is relatively small with a long palm and fairly short fingers, the longest phalange being the first. This shows her speedy grasp of an overall situation, ability to plan and organize. Malcolm's life line follows fairly closely around Venus, although there is a more adventurous outward movement in its latter stages, plus a new home to come. Sasha's leaves Venus for pastures new at about the age of forty-two. Sasha's head line is more deeply marked and has a branch below in addition to an extra head line above. Malcolm's is finer but *is almost exactly the same shape* including the branch, but it does not have the extra upper head line. Malcolm's heart line shows a strong line of non-communication and a heavy girdle of Venus above. Sasha's heart line is fairly clear, but it ends almost at the top of the hand on Jupiter. They both have the c section of the girdle showing the need to communicate with like-minded people and they can both become intellectually immersed in what they are doing.

The astrologers among you might like to note that Malcolm has the Sun and Moon in the eighth house in Pisces with Leo rising. Sasha has the Sun in Leo in the fourth house, the Moon in Pisces in the tenth house and Gemini rising. Both of us are creative, proud of our achievements, humorous and communicative—as well as being moody, sarcastic and critical of ourselves and others.

# CHAPTER FOURTEEN

# THE SPIRITUAL SIDE OF LIFE

We tend to view spiritual life as something that has little or nothing to do with our normal everyday lives. While it is true that we must live in the material world, make a living, look after our families and do our normal workaday chores, there is no need for us to reject all but the things that we can experience with our basic five senses. The spiritual, psychic and unseen worlds are with us all the time, whether we are tuned into this or not. Whether we are aware of it or not, we all have a spiritual aspect to our lives. Just as we live and learn in our normal daily lives, so our spirits also grow and learn— often through meeting, mingling and blending with other people's auras.

We are all aware that we carry a electromagnetic aura around us. All we need do to see this in action is to stand in a dark room and remove a sweater manufactured from man-made fiber after a day of walking around in it. The aura is something like this field, but it extends much further, so that it can easily touch the auras, and even the bodies of those who we mix with during the course of any day. Sometimes when we meet a new person, we instantly take to them, but on other times we can feel uncomfortable. Most people have a neutral effect on us, so that we are neither inexplicably drawn to them nor unnerved by them. Sometimes when we meet someone who we like straight off, when we get into conversation with them, we find that we have spent time in the same place at some date in the past, even though we didn't know each other at the time. Even when this is not the case, there is such a feeling of kinship, that it is clear that we definitely have spent time together, but not in this lifetime!

## Healing (Fig 14.1)

Next time you have the benefit of being around a healer who is working, take a look at his hands when he is through, because you

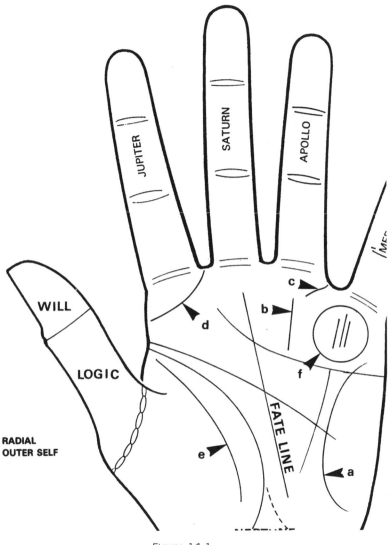

Figure 14.1

may notice a brown shadow that is visible under the health line. This shadow will disappear after a few minutes.

The mount of Neptune is located at the base of the hand, immediately above the wrist rascettes. This links the conscious, every day world with the unconscious, spiritual world. A healer needs to cross this in order to open his chakras (spiritual energy centers).

## The Kanda Ethereal Triangle (Fig 14.2)

Kanda is a Sanskrit word that refers to the ethereal triangle at the base of the spine that stores the energy of the Sushumna. This will work its way up the Kundalini as one evolves.

Take a look at the Kanda Ethereal Triangle and you will see that the mount of Neptune corresponds to the lower end of the spinal column, and thus to the seat of healing energy. It then links with the line of Mars, the health line and the life line to form a triangle of spiritual energy. It is interesting that the life line also represents the spinal chord. This means that it can be read in two ways, either as an indicator of the health of the physical spine but also in association with the chakras that are aligned along its length and also those of the skull.

The mount of Neptune is connected in some way with the brain and nervous system. To an astrologer, it would make sense to call this a second Mercury area. However, while Mercury is concerned with daily life, in both palmistry and astrology, Neptune is associated with meditation, healing and higher levels of consciousness. Neptune allows us to tap into this when we need to do so. Those who develop spiritually will have lines that split off from the life line and that end up in this Neptune area.

## The Line of Mars (Fig. 14.1e)

This line denotes protection in life and in sickness, and it does not appear in every person's hands. If the line flows towards the mount of Neptune, the subject will be aware of his spiritual path and he will tend to follow it. Even if he leaves the pathway for a while, things will happen to bring him back to it.

## Healing Striate (Fig. 14.1f)

The healing striate are located on the mount of Mercury. This makes astrological sense as Mercury is one of the gods of healing and is associated with the health-conscious sign of Virgo. When healing striate

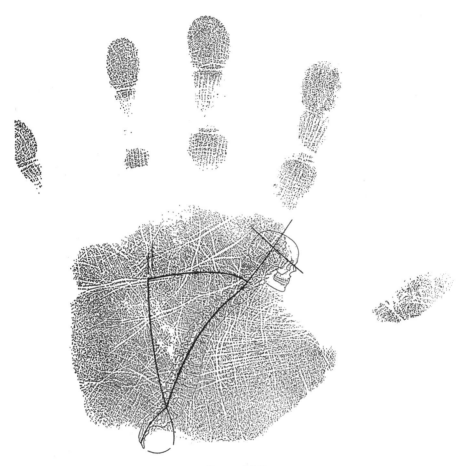

Figure 14.2

only appear on the minor hand, the person has healing ability but life, circumstances and those who he has had to deal with throughout his life have taken him on a path that did not involve him in healing. This can indicate that he has a desire to help and heal others but that somehow he missed this particular bus—at least in this lifetime. This may be the mark of a young soul who has yet to find his spiritual pathway. When the striate appear on the major hand (or on both) this shows that by mingling with the auras of others, and perhaps by being irrevocably drawn to the world of healing, the person will spend some part of his lifetime actively engaged in the pursuit.

- Three slightly diagonal lines are the most common kind of healing striate. Often these are crossed by another line that passes through each of them in a diagonal direction. One line in this area suggests that the subject can work alone. More than one line suggests that the person handle his patients in a one-on-one fashion.
- Many fine lines suggest that he work in a group or in concert with others. A line that touches the heart line and another that touches the lower end of the Mercury finger belongs to a communicator and teacher. If a line creeps up into the inner corner of the Mercury finger, he is psychic.
- A long fork on the Apollo side suggests that this subject saves lives, and so he may work in an accident and emergency ward, intensive care or as a surgeon or even as a spiritual healer.
- A long line with a Y formation on the top belongs to those who work with or who are associated with those who are terminally sick. Their unconscious task is to "lift souls" and to help them pass from this world to the next. This formation can be seen on the hands of those who care for the very old and very sick. Sometimes this line indicates a person who is not afraid to be with or to comfort the dying, and thus he is the person who tends to be with family members and others towards the end of their lives.
- A long fork on the percussion side, near to the attachment lines, shows that the person cares for children, and this subject may be a midwife or a child-care worker, a social worker or police officer who specializes in helping children or a child psychologist. Alternatively, he may foster or adopt children or help them as a scout master, in a sporting capacity or in some other way.

Look at the mount of Mercury and cordon it off into an imaginary square. Healing striate on the percussion side indicate caring for family members and caring for children.

- On the Apollo side, this also suggests someone who takes a caring role in the home but who also cares for others and who may work in the field of medicine or spiritual healing.
- If the striate are close to (or run into) the base of the Mercury finger, the person will be a communicator, writer, teacher, psychic and clairvoyant.

- If they are close to or touching the heart line, the person will put his heart into what he does and may wish to be the leader or organizer of a group.

## Psychism on the hand

The following are all signs of psychism, so even one of these marks will enhance intuition, but more than one or two features signify a psychic gift.

- A full mount of Neptune.
- A long, sloping head line especially if it has a looped skin ridge pattern somewhere below the end part of it.
- A curved line of intuition *(Fig. 14.1a)* on the percussion side of the health line, either on the mount of Luna or curving right up from Luna towards the heart line.
- A double loop or whorl on the Jupiter finger or the thumb. Busy hands that show mental energy rather than empty ones that denote a more physical type of nature.

## And Finally ... (Figs. 14.3 and 14.4)

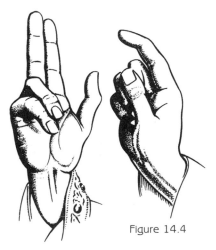

Malcolm's beautiful illustrations, that he has taken from Van Eyck's paintings demonstrate the religious outlook and the political outlook. Both hands keep their private side of life hidden, but in both cases these leaders display their working lives clearly.

The religious leader is happily showing us his Jupiter finger of ego and leadership, and his Saturn finger of religion, science and deep thought—along with the practicalities of doing rather well in life. The worldly leader wants us to be aware of his ego and opinions (Jupiter), and also his

Figure 14.4

Figure 14.3

willpower and logical mind (the thumb), but anything that constitutes his private life is hidden. The fact that his Saturn finger is also hidden tells us that he is less sure of his future status or indeed, his future standard of living.

# INDEX